DREAMING WITH THE ARCHANGELS

DREAMING WITH THE ARCHANGELS

A Spiritual Guide to Dream Journeying

LINDA MILLER-RUSSO
PETER MILLER-RUSSO

WEISER BOOKS
Boston, MA/York Beach, ME

First published in 2002 by
Red Wheel/Weiser, LLC
368 Congress Street
Boston, MA 02210
www.redwheelweiser.com

Library of Congress Cataloging-in-Publication Data

Miller-Russo, Linda.
    Dreaming with the archangels : a spiritual guide to dream journeying /
Linda Miller-Russo, Peter Miller-Russo.
        p. cm.
    ISBN 1-57863-252-8 (pbk. : alk. paper)
    1. Archangels—Miscellanea. 2. Dreams—Miscellanea. 3. Spiritual life.
I. Miller-Russo, Peter II. Title.

    BF1999 .M686 2002
    135'.3—dc21

                                                                2001046785

Typeset in Galliard

Printed in Canada

TCP

08 07 06 05 04 03 02
 7 6 5 4 3 2 1

*To Linda's mother, Lucille, whose passion for dream study inspired
Linda from an early age to look to her dreams
as a source of self-knowledge and wisdom.*

Contents

Acknowledgments

The Circle of Angelic Enlightenment was founded through the inspiration of the four archangels: Michael, Raphael, Gabriel, and Uriel. These four form the foundation of the Circle of Angels. We thank them for their guidance.

We also thank the following people for the parts they played in helping us complete this work:

- Jen, for her love of books and for her encouragement and support in all of our projects.
- Angelo, whose determination to *not* read our books motivates us to write even more.
- Kathy (from the Presence of Angels), for her choice to believe in us.
- Bob Miller, for your enthusiasm and praise of our writing—it means more to us than you'll ever know.
- Rev. Carolyn White, our good friend, for sharing her many gifts with us and for her appreciation of all that we do.
- Tim Davis, for the pride in your voice when you told us how much you enjoyed finding our book in the bookstores. We miss you and we will remember you always.
- Caroline Pincus (Book Midwife/Editor), whose dedication to the art of writing inspired and encouraged us during the process of creating (and re-creating) this book.
- Jan Johnson (Publisher), for her vision of what this book could be and for giving us the opportunity to present it to people throughout the world.

"And these are the names of the holy angels who watch.

"Uriel, one of the holy angels, who is over the world and over Tartarus.

"Raphael, one of the holy angels, who is over the spirits of men...

"Michael, one of the holy angels, to wit, he that is set
over the best part of mankind and over chaos...

"Gabriel, one of the holy angels, who is over Paradise
and the serpents and the Cherubim..."

—ENOCH I:1–8

PART I

Dreaming with the Archangels

A person is disposed to an act of choice
by an angel ... in two ways. Sometimes,
a man's understanding is enlightened by
an angel to know what is good, but it is
not instructed as to the reason why....

But sometimes he is instructed by angelic
illumination, both that this act is good
and as to the reason why it is good.

—ST. THOMAS AQUINAS, *THE BLISS OF THE WAY*

CHAPTER 1

Dreaming with the Archangels

The four archangels—Michael, Raphael, Gabriel, and Uriel—invite you to join them on a special thirty-day journey, one unlike any you have taken before. Instead of traveling to a foreign country, over land or sea, you'll journey with the archangels into the spiritual frontier of your own dream worlds. During this journey you will have many unique opportunities. You may meet with each of the four archangels in their spiritual bodies to receive their guidance and wisdom; contact and converse with your deceased loved ones in the afterlife; uncover your life's mission by connecting to your soul self; tap into past lifetimes; or dream of future waking-world events.

Important historic events have been heralded and even shaped by dreams. The Bible contains some of these important dream references. Specifically, consider the tragedy that Joseph avoided when he heeded the angel-inspired dream to flee Bethlehem just as King Herod gave the order to murder all newborn male children:

> "...behold, the angel of the Lord appeareth to Joseph in a dream, saying, Arise, and take the young child and his mother, and flee into Egypt, and be thou there until I bring thee word: for Herod will seek the young child to destroy him. When he arose, he took the young child and his mother by night, and departed into Egypt: And was there until the death of Herod: that it might be fulfilled which was spoken of the Lord by the prophet, saying, Out of Egypt have I called my son." —Matt 2:13–15

If Joseph had not learned to understand and trust the guidance of his dreams, the course of history would have changed dramatically. The present that we know would probably not exist. Just as these history-altering dreams are important to the course of humanity, so too are our personal dreams critical in helping us chart the course of our lives.

The Benefits of the Dream Worlds

Dreams are special in that they are not limited to the rules of the physical world. The blind can see in their dreams, the lame walk, the hurt receive healing, and the dead can speak to us through unseen channels that connect each of us to the mystery of our existence. This nonrestrictive quality of the dream environment provides us with the opportunity to have experiences that we cannot have while in our waking state.

The temporary nature of the constraints found within the dream worlds thus offers us several advantages over waking-world experiences. First, in dreams we can take more risks than we can in the physical world. We may choose to fly, to do battle, to drive fast or in dangerous conditions. We can also choose to face the hidden parts of ourselves within our dreams. In fact, repressed parts of ourselves use the dream worlds as a pressure relief valve. They use archetypal symbols as their language, as they express their needs and concerns to our conscious mind.

Solving Problems

Dreams offer us a virtual environment for experimentation. Similar to the waking state's imaginative faculty, dreams give us a wonderful opportunity to immerse ourselves in a 3-D world in order to learn and solve problems. Many famous inventors have reportedly received answers in their dreams to perplexing problems regarding their physical experiments and work. You too can use dream worlds to assist you in solving your waking-state problems, both at work and at home, in relationships and in pursuit of the betterment of humanity.

Exploring Personal Issues

Dreams provide an excellent place to explore our personal life issues. They give us the opportunity to safely delve into sensitive areas of our personal and work relationships with loved ones and others without incurring lasting or detrimental physical effects. In dreams, we don't have to hold back for fear of hurting or alienating others. Much healing can and does occur in our dream worlds because it is safe to vent the full range of our feelings there.

For example, when Linda went through a divorce, she did much of her healing in her dream worlds. There she could fully explore and express her feelings of anger, rejection, and fear. The dream character that represented Linda's ex-husband not only listened to her express her feelings, but he also acknowledged the validity of her pain. Thus, the characters within Linda's dreams actually took a clear and active role in promoting her emotional healing during that difficult time. Our dreams will sustain and nurture us, if only we agree to listen to the healing messages that they contain. This is precisely one of the goals of the thirty-day dream journey: to help us tune in to the wisdom contained in our dreams.

The Four Archangels

The four archangels are the driving force as well as the wisdom bearers for your thirty-day dream journey. Just as they have used the dream state to deliver the messages and guidance of God to men and women throughout history, they now offer each of us this unique opportunity to journey with them into the dream worlds.

Each of the archangels distributes a unique energy stream that will assist us in our unfoldment:

- **Michael,** archangel of truth, honesty, and justice, stresses that we must tell ourselves the total truth to the greatest extent that we can, day by day. He helps us to expand our consciousness by removing redundant and self-limiting energy patterns so that we can begin to move out of old paths and disempowering relationships. Many times the movement is not physical but rather a matter of internal attitude. Becoming locked within a specific viewpoint can prevent us from gaining the experiences we need in order to make our mark upon the world.

- **Raphael,** archangel of healing, wholeness, and acceptance, shows us that we must move from repression of our true feelings to the full, complete, and healing expression that comes from the purity within our hearts. According to this glorious healing angel, we must face our pain head-on and learn to drill below surface layers of emotion in order to connect with the tender core of our being.

    The shell we unconsciously place around our heart as a protection from pain unwittingly becomes a prison that also locks away our dreams. We have forgotten that the key to unlocking our deepest dreams lies within our reach. Raphael teaches that the process of expressing our inner feelings dissolves restrictive energy patterns so that our dreams can freely manifest in the world around us.

- **Gabriel,** archangel of strength, commitment, and persistence, stresses that we can accomplish our chosen life mission only through dedicated commitment and persistence. If we fail to achieve our goals not only will we suffer, but our family, friends, and the community of earth will suffer as well. Gabriel teaches that we are each important and that we are each interconnected with each other. Therefore what we do and what we do *not* do in our lives does matter!

  This powerful messenger of God will help us to define and carry out our life's mission. This is his area of expertise. He has been dispatched by the Lord to deliver to us, in clear terms, the knowledge and the blueprint that our soul has established for this lifetime on Earth.

- **Uriel,** archangel of love, beauty, and awareness, states that when we appreciate life, we shine the light of infinite love upon all. As we appreciate, we radiate an inner warmth from the core of our being that soothes and heals all with whom we come into contact.

  He reminds us that while we are busy reconstructing our realities with Michael, recovering our inner selves with Raphael, and defining our life's mission with Gabriel, we must also take time to just "be." The exercise of "being" recharges us and keeps us connected to God's infinite energy. This is the state of being that yogis, sages, and masters have tried to impart to us since the beginning of human history. Uriel teaches that this state is available—here and now.

During your dreams and meditations, you may experience the archangels and their respective energy streams, collectively or individually, as a feeling of peace, strength, and love. You may also experience them in their angelic forms, illuminated by the holy flame of God's omnipotent presence.

Rediscovering the Secrets of the Dream Worlds

In today's society, dreams are looked at not as sources of wisdom but rather as odd and strange imaginings of the murky subconscious mind. In the process of devaluing our dream worlds we have, for the most part, lost the secret knowledge and art of dream interpretation. But this was not always the case.

Think of ancient times; what image comes to mind—the pyramids in Egypt, the glorious temples of Greece, the ruins of the Atlantean empire? What do these civilizations all have in common? These magnificent empires, when at their apex, each had a deep awareness and appreciation for dream world exploration. Dream oracles, as guardians of the dream portals, routinely gave their wisdom both to rulers and to the common people. Teaching masters walked the roads, accessible to their disciples and to the general populace. They taught the basic methods of dream interpretation to all those interested. The people of the time faced concerns of immediate survival and the fulfillment of their hopes and dreams; understanding the language of the dream worlds was of critical importance, for it provided them with answers to their life problems.

As humanity has progressed through the ages, we have begun to rely more on what we have created than on seeking to understand the Creator. But there is hope for those who see the value of learning to understand the messages of the inner worlds that come to us through dream world channels. We are fortunate that the four archangels, the divine messengers of God, have spearheaded an effort to return this sacred knowledge to us once again. In fact, dream study is an integral part of the archangels' plan of healing, the essence of which is to instruct each of us on how to fully process our experiences in order to live in a state of conscious connection to the life stream known as the Holy Spirit—with a heart open to life.

As beings of pure spirit, the archangels use the dream worlds to deliver messages and guidance that will lead us to the light of God and to the wisdom of our soul. Armed with their thirty-day dream journey program and fueled by a desire to learn and grow, you are now in a position to uncover the divine plan of your soul—your reason for being.

Thirty-Day Focus

Dreaming with the Archangels is divided into two main parts. The first part (chapters 1 through 3) will help you to prepare for your thirty-day dream journey. Here you will learn how to purify your consciousness so that you can better receive angelic visions and communications. This section offers practical steps on *how to remember your dreams* and *how to interpret your dreams.* You will also learn how to create a personal dream journal to record your experiences during your journey.

The second part of the book contains the thirty-day dream journey. Each evening during this journey you will review a special dream topic and perform a technique that will stimulate specific dream experiences. The next morning, guided by one of the four archangels, you'll record your dream experiences and unseal their hidden messages. After completing all thirty days of your journey, you will have taken a major step toward self-integration and illumination by focusing the light of your awareness upon your dream worlds.

Why Start Now?

Are you at a stalemate in your spiritual growth? Do you need answers to pressing life problems? Have you given up on trying to figure out the hidden messages of your dreams? If so, then you owe it to yourself to take a thirty-day dream journey with the four archangels. They will lead you to a deep and penetrating understanding of your inner worlds. At the end of the thirty days you will have transformed the third of your life you spend sleeping into an exciting adventure of personal growth and transformation. Join us now!

CHAPTER 2

Preparing for Your Dream Journey

Preparing for a dream journey is as important as preparing for a physical journey. Just as you would make preparations for a trip to Europe, such as finalizing travel arrangements, purchasing a travel guide, and packing your suitcase, you need to prepare yourself for your dream journey with the archangels. This preparation comes in two main areas: inner (spiritual) and outer (physical).

The first part of this chapter shows you how you can deepen your connection to the angels by taking steps to purify your inner consciousness. The second part provides information on how to create a sacred outer environment for your dream study, including ideas on creating a dream journal and dedicating a sacred space in your home for a devotional altar.

Inner World Preparation

The information that follows will help you strengthen your connection to angelic realms through the purification of your consciousness.

The Importance of Purifying Your Consciousness

Purification helps us lift ourselves from the concerns and density of the physical world to the higher, finer (light-filled) frequencies of the heaven worlds. As our consciousness is lifted and purified, it becomes a clear channel through which inspiration from the angelic realms can flow.

To make the connection to the higher energies, we must cleanse our consciousness of the painful residue and self-centeredness that block the light of God from filtering through. We can accomplish this through self-examination (processing our experiences) and by focusing on spiritual practices.

This purification of self—heart, mind, and soul (feelings, thoughts, intentions)—creates a space for the light and grace of God to fill, bringing blessings and miracles into the lives of everyone involved. Our interactions with each other begin to flow from a point of love and connection, rather than from fear and separation. Connection creates a loving communion with others, and in this state of communion, messages flow undistorted from the Godhead to humanity—via the Creator's holy angels.

You may already devote personal time to inner spiritual practices, such as prayer work, meditation, and contemplation. If so, you are already lifting and purifying your consciousness. You may simply wish to use the information in this section to refresh yourself on the importance of devotional work and to reinforce your commitment to ongoing spiritual purification.

Purification and Angelic Communications

Many saints communicated with God and the angels. Often they received information in the dream state. At other times they received information while awake, in what they called "communications" or "visions."

For example, St. Teresa of Avila (A.D. 1582) reported receiving "interior communications" from God that were often accompanied by raptures and ecstatic states. She reported that during one of these communications she heard, within her soul, these words, "I will not have you hold conversation with men, but with Angels." St. Teresa reported that these interior communications were more distinct and clear than human speech, and that the joy and peace of these communications inspired her soul to strong sentiments of virtue. She went on to establish many Carmelite convents.

The Catholic community and her fellow Carmelite nuns deeply respected St. Teresa's spiritual connection to God. Indeed, the Carmelite nuns who worked closely with her reported many instances when they had the privilege of witnessing her levitating during her rapturous communications with God.

Remember, you don't have to be a saint to communicate with God and the angels. Most of the saints saw themselves as great sinners, and thus they worked very hard in their daily lives (through prayer, meditation, caring for the sick, and so on) to be worthy of the graces that God bestowed upon them.

If you have trouble believing that you can, indeed, have direct spiritual contact with angelic beings and receive their messages in the dream worlds, consider the technology of a simple television set. This human creation is a modern miracle that we often take for granted—for out of nothing but thin air, images and sounds travel at incredible speeds across vast distances and appear for our viewing.

In much the same manner that a television set receives images transmitted through the air, you can be the receiver for transmissions from the spiritual realms. When looked at this way, communicating with the spiritual realms is no more a creation of the imagination than is viewing images of the physical worlds on your television set.

While we do not need to become saints to commune with God, we are wise to follow their example. A purified, prayerful consciousness can better tune into the loving messages sent to us by God and His angels. The spiritual practices used by the saints—prayer, positive intentions, contemplation, and meditation—increase our receptivity to God's "channel."

Prayer as a Sacred Tool of Inner Purification

In prayer we talk to God. We share with Him our innermost thoughts and feelings. We sort through our confusion, fears, and misunderstandings. This self-examination cleanses us, and as we become cleansed, we can better clarify our intentions in each situation as well as specify our hopes for the future. We ask for understanding and for forgiveness.

We then ask God for healing. We ask Him to send His light and grace to us, to help us in our every endeavor. We pray to Him for the strength and courage to be honest and loving in our relationships, and to fulfill all of our responsibilities with integrity and grace. Prayer also gives us the opportunity to ask God to extend His grace and blessings to our loved ones and to others in need.

Prayers are like love letters to ourselves and to God. They help us define who we are and who we want to become. They function as a guideline to the development of soul. Take the time to write your heartfelt prayers in a prayer journal. Use them daily to attune your consciousness and heart to the spiritual realms. By doing this you will prepare a space in your inner worlds for the angels to reside over the course of your dream journey. You can use the following prayer to prepare your consciousness for the journey ahead. Recite it silently to yourself right now.

Prayer of Preparation

Dear God,

I prepare my consciousness to receive your communications through your divine messengers, the archangels. I desire to be more loving and caring—to be that which you created me to be. I ask this in Jesus' name. Amen.

Meditation as a Sacred Tool of Inner Purification

In prayer we talk to God; in meditation we listen to God. By stilling the chatter of our conscious mind, we put ourselves into a balanced, receptive state where the creative mind of God can communicate with us. Just as we can receive messages and visions in our dreams, so too can we receive insights and impressions from the mind of God during meditation.

This meditative connection to our core essence (the essence of God) aids us in accessing the wisdom stored in our higher self. As we tap into this wisdom, we become more aware of the directives of our soul self, which in turn helps us to manifest our chosen mission for this lifetime.

The calming influence of meditation benefits the entire body system. On the psychological front, meditation can provide respite from strong energies, such as worry, anxiety, and sadness. When we meditate, we align ourselves with a state of peace, akin to the calm found in the eye of a storm. From this position we can regain our balance and solidify our sense of connection to the source of strength within us.

Take a few minutes now to perform the following short meditation. It will help prepare you for your journey with the archangels.

Meditation in Preparation for Your Journey

Close your eyes and relax. Allow your thoughts to meander, like a flowing stream in the forest. Follow your thoughts as they float downstream. As you do, notice the tall trees and the beautiful blue sky above the canopy of the forest. After a short time the stream ends, and you find yourself (and your thoughts) in a shimmering pool of water. This water is different. You can feel it cleanse you and transform your thoughts, extracting all that is good within them and healing all that is hurt. Open your eyes and know that you have taken a step to prepare for your dream journey with the archangels by purifying your thoughts.

The End Result

After purifying our hearts through prayer, meditation, and self-examination we become minutely aware of being *immersed* in a sea of spirit. Each action seems directed not only by a part of us, but also by life itself. This creates within us a feeling of "right" action—a state of inner certainty, contentment, and fulfillment. Immersed in this sea of spirit, we view every action with compassion, and we realize that our every movement is being synchronized and choreographed by God's love, in absolute harmony and for the good of all. Our consciousness is now purified, and we are ready to receive angelic communications.

Outer World Preparation

The following information will help you to create a sacred environment for your dream world exploration.

Creating the Thirty-Day Dream Journal

During each day of your journey you will record your dreams, insights, and interpretations in a dream journal. You want this to be a very special book, because by using it daily, you will be creating a literal map of the inner realms and your dream worlds.

We strongly suggest that you create your own journal. In doing so you acknowledge the sacredness of your journey and give meaning to the experiences of your daily life. Each day that you choose to write in your journal will become a day of renewal and rededication to living your life as a process—appreciating and learning from your experiences.

You can create your journal by purchasing some inspiring stationery (preferably lined sheets) and using a three-hole punch and fasteners to bind at least thirty pages together. An art print or a photograph of a person or place that has spiritual significance for you can make a great cover. (You can mount your chosen image on card stock if desired.) Choose something that calls to your soul—something that reminds you of the reality of your spiritual journey.

Here are some cover ideas:

- a photo or art print of a church, cathedral, or temple
- a photo or art print of the Swiss Alps or the Himalayan mountains
- your favorite prayer, quotation, or poem
- a print of the angels by an old master (Raphael, Titian)
- a print of a spiritual teacher you admire (Jesus, Mother Teresa, the Dalai Lama, Padre Pio)
- one of your own special photos

Of course if you are pressed for time, you can simply purchase a blank book. But try to find one that feels special to you, or make it special by decorating it with an image of personal significance.

We cannot overstress the importance of using your journal. It is an integral part of the archangels' thirty-day dream journey. Journaling stimulates dream awareness and personal growth by making us aware of the patterns and issues that shape our life in the waking world. Our dreams reflect these waking-world issues back to us each night in their colorful mini-dramas. By recording our dreams, thoughts, and feelings, we create an expanding record of insights that will facilitate our journey to wholeness.

Remember, your journal is like the doorway to your soul's purpose—commit yourself to opening and using it often.

Creating an Altar (A Sacred Space)

An altar in your home represents the flowering of God's presence within you. It also serves as a focal point through which your inner devotional qualities can expand and grow. While this step is optional we strongly recommend that you prepare a special physical space for your meditations, prayer work, and dream journaling.

Whenever we devote ourselves to spiritual practices, a high vibrational energy field is created. Just as a church or meditation center develops a strong spiritual energy vortex through the devotion of the people who gather there, so too will you create a spiritual energy field in the altar space where your spiritual work is centered. Use the following steps to create, bless, and dedicate your altar:

1. Choose and Cleanse Your Altar Space

Choose an uncluttered part of your home and claim it as your very own. Even a small corner or a closet will do if space is limited. Locate this sacred altar space in a quiet area of your home, if possible. Fully cleanse your space, both spiritually and physically. To perform a spiritual cleansing of the space, follow these steps:

- Light a white candle in the center of your altar space (use a fire-safe candle holder). The flame represents the ever-burning love that God has for you, and the white candle represents the pure healing light of God.

- Place an incense burner next to the white candle, and light cleansing incense, such as sandalwood, Nag Champa, or frankincense. Again, make sure you use a fire-safe incense burner.

- Then speak out loud the following prayer, infusing your words with your desire to honor God and to grow spiritually:

Dear God,
*   May your healing white light surround and enfold this*
sacred altar space, sealing it from all darkness and negativity.
May it be a place of purity and peace where your inspiration
and grace can easily be received. Amen.

2. Choose an Altar

Once you have cleansed the space you have chosen for your altar, it is time to choose what form your altar will take. A cardboard box covered with a beautiful altar cloth works just fine. Or, you can use a small wooden table. Make your altar as simple or as ornate as you wish.

You may choose to cover your altar with a cloth or to carve spiritual symbols or quotations upon it. You might decoupage a religious print of a spiritual being, such as an angel, upon your altar.

3. Choose Devotional Articles

The next step is to choose the devotional articles you wish to place on your altar. For example, if you are Christian, you would likely place the Holy Bible, a picture of Jesus, and perhaps a book of prayers upon it. If you are Buddhist, you might choose a book of Buddhist meditations and some photos of Buddhist masters. Placing angel pictures and statues upon your altar helps to welcome them into your home. You might also wish to welcome your favorite saints in the same way.

A beautiful plant or flowers on your altar honors God for the beauty of His creation. Other good additions include candles and incense. "Breathing in" the fragrances released by candles and incense can help attune your consciousness to higher spiritual frequencies as well as to formerly experienced altered states of consciousness.

4. Bless and Dedicate Your Altar

Once you have arranged your chosen items on the altar, it is time to bless and dedicate the altar. Light the candles and incense, and say the following blessing as you stand before your altar:

> *Dear Creator God,*
> *Please bless and make my altar a sacred place for your holy*
> *presence. Please send your holy angels here to commune with me*
> *and inspire me as I lift myself up to you. This I ask through the*
> *universal Christ energy. Amen.*

To further sanctify your altar you may want to sprinkle it lightly with holy water (blessed water) as you say the following dedication:

> *I dedicate this altar to God who created me in His image. May*
> *my spiritual practice honor Him for His care and loving-kindness.*
> *May the angels and saints be ever present here to carry my prayers*
> *to the Lord and to seal His wisdom within my heart. Amen.*

Feel free to modify the blessing and dedication to reflect your particular spiritual practice and beliefs.

Your altar is now ready to use. Don't be afraid to add to or change the items on your altar as new symbols gain spiritual significance for you. Remember, you are an evolving spiritual being, and your altar should represent the changes and growth you experience.

Gathering Other Materials for Your Journey

Besides creating your dream journal and making a sacred space, you should have a few other items on hand before beginning your thirty-day dream journey with the archangels:

- a special or favorite pen to use with your journal
- three-by-five-inch index cards
- candles (three blue and three white safety candles—always extinguish candles after use)
- colored pencils or markers
- a small flashlight
- incense (optional)
- a tape recorder and blank tapes (optional)

The Next Step

You have taken steps to prepare your consciousness for spiritual contact with the angels. You have gathered the sacred tools you will need for your journey. Now you are ready to begin focusing on the dream worlds. The next chapter contains important "dream basics"—information that will help you gain the most from your dream journey with the archangels. It includes tips on remembering your dreams and a method you can use to interpret your dreams.

CHAPTER 3

Dreamwork Basics

Before you begin working with the archangels in the dream worlds, it's important that you review the following dreamwork "basics." These basics include tips on remembering your dreams and a special method for interpreting them. This information has been condensed from our study of the dream worlds over the past twenty years. It will help you lay the foundation for the specific work you will do with the archangels during your thirty-day journey.

Remembering Your Dreams

In order to work with our dream self we must first and foremost remember our dreams. Often we may wake up in the morning believing that we have not had any dreams. But it is more likely that we have *not yet remembered* the dreams we did indeed have. Think of the many times you have gotten up and dressed and gone off to work or school and then, out of the blue, recalled a dream experience. Such recall comes suddenly and for no apparent reason. This is one way our dreams come back to us.

Don't feel discouraged if you do not remember your dreams on awakening. Dream recall can come at any time during your day, and you can do many things to encourage better dream recall. We've put together a list of our favorite ten.

Key #1: Get Enough Restful Sleep

Most people need at least six to eight hours of uninterrupted sleep in order to experience the highest level of dream recall. We need to go through the ninety-minute sleep/dream cycle several times before we become rested enough to have a conscious memory of our dreams.

With some exceptions, most people who only get four or five hours of sleep each night short-circuit their natural dream cycle. Only you know exactly how sleep much you need. You might want to experiment several nights in a row to discover the optimum number of hours you need to obtain the clearest dream recall.

Key #2: Sleep with Your Head to the North

Sleeping with your head pointing true north puts your body and its corresponding chakra system in alignment with the polar magnetism of the earth. Yogi masters, mystics, and psychics have long recommended this position for healthful sleep. We have found that sleeping with our head to the north strengthens our connection to the higher, intuitive self; promotes the health of the body and the central nervous system; enhances restful sleep; and stimulates the highest and most vivid level of dream recall.

A simple compass can assist you in determining true north in your bedroom. Sleeping with your head to the other three compass directions will also affect your sleep experiences. For example, sleeping with your head to the south grounds you to the earth. This helps to reduce the occurrence of nightmares and invasive dreams. However, the downside of the south position is that it tends to dampen dream recall.

Key #3: Set Your Intentions with an Affirmation

We have discovered that what we pay attention to most often grows stronger and bears fruit. And so it is with dreams. Giving conscious attention to dreams will allow you to receive important messages of healing and wisdom that the hidden parts of you (subconscious, emotional, higher, and soul selves) are trying to bring to your attention every night.

It is especially helpful to use a simple, strongly worded affirmation of intention before you fall asleep at night. Try something like, "I will remember my dreams in the morning." Repeat this affirmation, or one similar to it, several times as you fall asleep.

Key #4: Keep Dream Tools Handy and Commit to Using Them Nightly

Acknowledge how serious you are about your dream worlds by keeping your dream journal or a tape recorder close to your bedside. Then make an inner commitment to *use* these tools each night. It also helps to have a small flashlight handy when recording your dreams; oftentimes turning on a bright light will drive your dream memories away. A bright light may also awaken you so much that you will find it difficult to fall back to sleep.

Key #5: Give Yourself Extra Time in the Morning

An obvious but sometimes overlooked aid to remembering your dreams is to simply set aside an extra fifteen minutes in the morning for remembering and recording your dreams. Set the alarm fifteen minutes earlier than usual or train yourself to wake earlier so that you don't have to jump out of bed in a rush to get ready for work or school.

Key #6: Keep Your Eyes Closed When You First Awaken

Another key to remembering your dreams is to *keep your eyes closed when you first awaken* to reduce the amount of external stimuli that normally floods your brain in the morning. It also provides a blank screen upon which your dream symbols, memories, and images can form. Finally, it promotes a state of relaxation that is beneficial when trying to access dream memories.

Keys #7 and 8: Relax and Be Still When You First Wake Up and Re-Create Your Dream in Reverse Sequence

Remember to keep your body as still as possible as you wake up. Wiggling, stretching, or sitting up can drive the memory of your dreams away just as quickly as a bright light can. Sometimes you may remember only one image or scene upon awakening. Don't worry! If you relax and lay still, you can often trace this one image backward and reconstruct your dream, frame by frame, from the last scene to the middle scenes and, eventually, to the beginning.

Key #9: Journal Your Feelings, Daydreams, and Fantasies Daily

Get into a daily habit of journaling your feelings, daydreams, and fantasies. You might be thinking: *I don't have time for this!* And it's true, many of us lead extremely busy lives and simply do not have a lot of extra time. But this type of journaling does not require a lot of extra time. Don't feel as if you need to record every event or thought of the day.

Simply jot down a paragraph or two (usually in the evening just before bed), describing any feelings, fantasies, or interesting thoughts you experienced that day. Even just a few words or key phrases will help trigger your memory of an idea or feeling you may want to explore later on. You will be rewarded with deep insights into your patterns and life processes when you connect your journal information to the issues being brought up in your dreams.

Dreams are internal manifestations of our thoughts, hopes, fears, and conflicts. They provide us with a stage upon which to examine our issues from the various viewpoints of our self-segments, and, most important, they often offer us creative solutions to dilemmas—solutions that have eluded our conscious mind.

Key #10: Create a Dream-Sharing Ritual

Create a morning dream ritual. Make it as simple or as complex as you choose. For example, Linda's mother created a morning dream ritual for her family simply by encouraging everyone to talk about his or her dreams during breakfast. Even if you live alone and have no built-in dream partners, you can still create meaningful rituals. One way is to bring your dreams to work and share them with an interested co-worker. You could also call or email a friend. The feedback we get from interested dream partners can provide valuable insights into our relationships and our inner psyches.

Although all the keys we have discussed are simple, they do require you to change. During your efforts to use these keys, don't become discouraged if you find it difficult to change your old habits to make time for the new activities outlined in the keys. Replacing old habits with new energy patterns is not easy. In order to be successful in changing your habits and installing a new pattern, your desire to work with your dream-self must be strong. The good news is that once you do establish a new pattern, it will become easier and easier for that pattern to take hold. Eventually it will become automatic, and you will gain all the benefit without great effort.

Study and refer to these ten tips as needed. You can use this chart to help refresh your memory during your thirty-day dream journey.

The Ten Keys to Remembering Your Dreams

1. Get enough restful sleep.
2. Sleep with your head to the north.
3. Set your intentions with an affirmation.
4. Keep dream tools handy and commit to using them nightly.
5. Give yourself extra time in the morning.
6. Keep your eyes closed when you first awaken.
7. Relax and be still when you first wake up.
8. Re-create your dream in reverse sequence.
9. Journal your feelings, daydreams, and fantasies daily.
10. Create a dream-sharing ritual.

Interpreting Your Dreams

As you interpret your dreams over the course of your thirty-day journey, you may find that they contain direct and literal communications from the angels, your spirit guides, and deceased loved ones. At other times the angels will influence your dream maker to provide you with dreams that contain encoded messages from your self-segments (the parts of your self, your component aspects, broken into parts for analysis and understanding).

Dreams that come from your self-segments can be viewed as plays or movies, complete with a cast of characters, props, settings, emotions, plots, action, and important dialogue. To understand and properly interpret them, you need to examine each of these elements.

We find the following seven-step process an efficient way of getting a remarkably complete dream interpretation.

1. Make an inventory or list of each of the characters that appear in your dream, both human and nonhuman.
2. Examine your feelings about the dream characters.
3. Examine your role in the dream and your relationships to the dream characters.
4. Review the actions taking place in the dream.
5. Find out what aspect of yourself the dream characters represent by engaging them in imaginary conversation.
6. Analyze the dream setting (location/time of day/environment).
7. Consider your current life situation.

Each of these steps is crucial to proper dream interpretation. Let's examine each in turn.

1. Make an Inventory of Characters

Who are the villains and the saints in your dreams? Why have they appeared in your dreams? What do they represent? Most likely they represent you. Or, more accurately, they represent a part of you, usually a part that is hidden from your conscious awareness, a part that wants to emerge and be recognized by you, the conscious self.

Sometimes your dream characters encapsulate a hurt or traumatized part of you, at other times they can represent a wisdom aspect of you such as your higher self. That's why the first step in interpreting a dream is to make an inventory of the characters that appear in it (both human and nonhuman).

Why are these different parts of you trying to emerge and gain your attention? While the surface reason may vary, the ultimate reason never does. The ultimate reason is simply this: *to promote the healing and wholeness of your psyche.*

Most of us have had dreams in which at least some of the following characters appeared: monster, sister, priest, brother, father, man with a knife, lover, mother, daughter, teacher, vampire, baby kitten, spouse, employer, doctor, soldier, actress, saint, witch, judge, angel, dog, friend, co-worker.

From the list above, pick three characters that have inhabited your dreamscapes. If none of these characters have appeared in your dreams, choose three others that have. Write them down in the spaces provided.

1. _____

2. _____

3. _____

2. Examine Your Feelings

The next step in the dream interpretation process is to determine your feelings toward the characters you uncovered in step one. With each character, ask yourself the following question: What are my *feelings* toward this character (fear, respect, a desire to nurture, anxiety, jealousy)?

Sometimes you may find it hard to identify exactly what or how you feel about a particular dream character. In such cases you may find it helpful to view the word not as a specific character from your dream but as a character in general. For example, let's say you picked the character "mother." What feelings are evoked when you read or hear that word? To further narrow it down, ask yourself about your feelings about your own mother, and finally, if it applies—how do you feel about being (or becoming) a mother?

Once you have identified your general feelings about the character, you can then look at the feeling that's evoked by the specific dream character. You can see that there may be myriad feelings to sort out. The better we know ourselves the easier it will be to discover the purpose and meaning of the characters that appear in our dreams.

3. Examine Your Role and Relationships

Next, you'll want to examine how you relate to the characters in your dreams. What was your role in the dream? What was your relationship to each character? For example, using the sample characters from step one above, were you cast in the dream as a *student* to the *teacher* character? Or as *director* to the *actress*? Or as *victim* to the *man with the knife*? What role did you play? The role that we play offers a significant key to interpreting the dream.

Sometimes our consciousness is not focused within any of the dream characters. It may seem as if we are floating above the drama, watching it unfold. That we are "watching life unfold" is in itself an important message to pay attention to. Whatever issue the drama depicts is the one that we are being "passive" about. This type of dream tells us that we need to examine this passive attitude and perhaps take some positive action.

4. Review the Actions

Lights—camera—*action!* Next you'll want to review the *actions* taken by the characters in your dream. These actions often reflect an issue you are dealing with (or should be examining) in your waking life. If someone was chasing you, for example, examine your life for an issue you are not facing. You may be literally "running away" from that issue.

The action in your dream can also reflect a need that is not getting met in your life. If you dream you are nursing a baby or caring for a tiny kitten, this might indicate a deep need to nurture—perhaps to nurture the innocent, childlike part of yourself. Alternatively, "nursing a baby" could symbolize your attitude toward a new project you've started and are trying to complete. In short, when trying to understand the actions taken by the characters in your dreams, always examine them in the context of your current issues and life situation.

5. Converse with Your Characters

This next step involves creating an imaginary dialogue between yourself and your dream characters. This process extends not only to the people and animals in your dream but also to inanimate objects, such as containers, windows, trees, tables, or utensils. In other words all the characters you've listed in step one. For example, if you listed a brown leather book as a character from your dream you might ask that book the following questions: Why have you appeared in my dream? What is your title? How does it feel to be a book? Why are you made out of brown leather? What can the pages inside you tell me about myself? Next, answer the questions as if *you* were the book. The idea is to take the point of view of as many of the characters in your dream as possible and have them dialogue with you and each other in order to gain as much information from them as you can.

The questions you ask your characters during this step should naturally lead you to other questions. Use your imagination here and allow yourself to "hear" the characters' responses to your questions. Follow-up questions will be likely based on their earlier responses. You may find this process odd, but it is possibly the most critical step in the dream interpretation process.

6. Analyze the Dream Setting

The sixth step is to define the dream setting and environment. For example, is the dream set outdoors, at your grandmother's house, at school, at work? This information tells you what time period in your life the dream issue is reflecting. For example, if you have a dream that takes place in your grandmother's home, you are likely being directed to examine a childhood issue.

The dream environment (weather, time of day, and so on) also contains important details to help you interpret your dream. For example, darkness signifies that you are not consciously aware of the core issue being brought up by your dream. A cloudy dreamscape denotes inner doubt about the dream situation or unresolved concerns or problems; a clear sky indicates a deep level of clarity and understanding of the elements within your dream.

7. Consider Your Current Life Situation

Our dreams often reflect issues that we struggle with in our daily life, therefore the seventh and final step requires that you consider your current life situation. Your dreams could very easily be offering you a creative solution to one or more problems as well as serving as a safe environment to vent and explore your feelings about some issue. As you interpret your dreams, reflect on any issues or problems you may have experienced over the past few days or weeks.

Upon completing the seven steps, the message of your dream should become more apparent to you. How do you know when you've reached the proper interpretation? As with anything in life that you're sure of, you'll have a strong feeling within you that you have properly received and understood the message. Also, the more time you spend practicing these steps and learning your unique symbology, the more you'll feel confident about your interpretation.

Dream Interpretation by the Numbers

The best way to illustrate the use of this technique to interpret dreams is to provide you with an example. Consider the following dream, which Peter had several years ago after he met and fell in love with Linda.

PETER'S "SHIP IN THE FOG" DREAM

> In the dream Linda and I were on a ship in the middle of the ocean. It was daytime and Linda was standing close to me as we looked out over the water. A heavy fog surrounded us, yet the ship kept a steady course as it moved forward. As we continued on our

journey, I said, "It's a good thing that this ship has electronic directional devices."

Interpreting the Dream

Now we will lead you through each step of the interpretation process.

Step 1. Make an Inventory of Characters

This step is straightforward. The following characters, both human *and* nonhuman, appeared in my dream:

Human Characters	Nonhuman Characters
Linda	Ship
Myself (Peter)	Heavy fog
	Ocean

Step 2. Examine Your Feelings

Examining my feelings about these characters, I uncovered the following:

Linda: Love and acceptance. Unlimited future growth.

Ship: Safe protection from the ocean surrounding Linda and me.

Fog: Excitement about what the fog was hiding from view.

Ocean: Awe at its immensity and depth.

Step 3. Examine Your Role and Relationships

In this dream my role was essentially that of a passenger. I simply enjoyed the view and allowed the ship to take Linda and me to its unknown destination.

Step 4. Review the Actions

Three main actions were present in my dream. The first action was the ship moving through the peaceful water. The second action was Linda and me looking out over the water. The final action was simply my comment about the ship's radar system.

Step 5. Converse with Your Characters

To create an imaginary dialogue with the dream characters, human and nonhuman, I began by asking each of the characters questions about themselves, allowing my imagination free reign as I "became" each one. I then answered the questions from their viewpoint. I wasn't concerned about right or wrong answers. The point at this stage was to gather as much information about the characters as I could.

Peter:	*Ship, what are you doing?*
Ship:	*I am taking you on a journey into your future.*
Peter:	*Why are you doing this?*
Ship:	*Because this is the nature of life, to move forward, always growing and always changing.*
Peter:	*When will we arrive?*
Ship:	*That depends on the direction that you order me to go. For although it seems that I am in control of your destination, it is you who control the compass.*
Peter:	*Fog, why are you covering my view?*
Fog:	*I am not covering your view, it is you who are choosing to live in the moment, seeing only that which is in front of you.*
Peter:	*What secrets do you hide from me?*
Fog:	*Nothing that you do not already know.*
Peter:	*Ocean, why am I sailing upon you?*
Ocean:	*I represent the worlds of emotion. You are in direct contact with your feeling nature.*
Peter:	*Your surface is peaceful and calm, will you begin to storm and rage?*
Ocean:	*I reflect your internal nature. Now you are in a state of calm acceptance of your life as it is in this moment.*

Step 6. Analyze the Dream Setting

My sample dream was set somewhere in the middle of the ocean surrounded by thick fog. I felt unable to just get up and leave the setting. Yet I felt no fear or desire to change the situation. I could not see where the ship was going, nor did I feel that I had the power to steer the ship to shore. I took this to mean that my life was on the move and I was in transition from one stage of life to another.

Step 7. Consider Your Current Life Situation

Now that I have examined all the elements *within* the dream, it is time to look at the circumstances and activities of my waking world. This step helps to put all the pieces of the dream into a meaningful perspective.

At the time that I had this dream, I had been separated from my now ex-wife for six months, and had just met Linda at a spiritual event. Linda and I became friends right away. The process of disengaging from my former marriage was traumatic yet exciting because of the possibilities opening to me. I had no idea how my future would pan out. I was truly living one day, even one moment, at a time.

Putting It All Together—the Dream Message

By pulling together the information from each of the seven steps, I came up with the following interpretation for my "ship in the fog" dream.

The ocean represents life itself. The action of the ship moving through the water symbolized the journey that Linda and I were embarking upon. The fact that the dream was set in the daytime indicates that I was consciously aware of the issue that the dream focused on—the journey of my life. The thick fog represented the undiscovered nature of my relationship with Linda and of our future together. Yet even though Linda and I were not sure where we were heading, I knew that the ship was being guided by some sort of electronic device (i.e., spirit, or our soul selves), for I felt no fear. Instead of fear I felt only a sense of adventure and trust in life.

During your thirty-day dream journey you will use these same seven steps to interpret your dreams. While it's important to understand the basics of the technique, there's no need to memorize the steps; we will repeat them for you throughout the dream journey. And if at any time you need additional clarification and guidance, you can always refer back to this chapter.

Working with dreams in this way does take some time and effort, yet we have found that the end results are well worth it. By probing your dreams fully, you will find yourself becoming closer to your own dream maker and your other self-segments—including your soul self. This attunement to your soul may well motivate you to delve ever more deeply into your inner realms through dream study and interpretation.

PART II

The Archangels' Thirty-Day Dream Journey

———

"For He shall give his Angels charge over you
to keep you in all your ways.
In their hands, they shall bear you up,
lest you dash your foot against a stone."

—PSALMS 91:11–12

CHAPTER 4

The Thirty-Day Dream Journey

Over the next thirty days you will find yourself led on a journey of transformation and personal growth—empowered by self-understanding and filled with the light of your soul. Each evening you'll read an informative passage that contains a specially designed dream technique for you to use. The next morning you'll review and interpret your evening's dreams. At the end of thirty days, you'll review what you've written and summarize what you've discovered about yourself, the dream worlds, and life itself.

During your thirty-day dream journey the four archangels will guide you as you learn to consciously process and decipher your dream messages. Michael will help you see the patterns and energies that play upon your dream worlds. Raphael will gently urge you to expression, helping you to keep your heart open to the Holy Spirit. Gabriel's dynamic energy will assist you in overcoming fear and self-doubt by filling you with hope and purpose. And Uriel will help you focus your consciousness on the eternal presence of the Creator with gratitude and appreciation for the divine plan of life.

The Purpose of the Thirty-Day Journey

The four archangels, under the direction of Archangel Michael, will guide you step by step through your dream worlds. Each day's dream material builds upon and expands the previous night's session. By focusing exclusively on your dream worlds for thirty consecutive days you will create a strong and powerful vortex for the energy of God to flow to you through His divine messengers, the archangels. At the end of the thirty-day program your dream worlds will be illuminated by the power and wisdom of your soul. Your newfound ability to tap into this wisdom will enable you to fulfill your part in the divine plan—your purpose for this lifetime.

The topics of your thirty-day journey have been arranged so that a particular Archangel will lead you in his area of expertise for several nights in a row. This will help attune you to that angel's energy and presence. The thirty days of your dream journey are structured as follows:

Days One through Seven: Archangel Michael

The first seven days of your journey are led by Michael, archangel of truth, honesty, and justice (the one exception, day 2, is led by Archangel Uriel). As the chief of the archangels, Michael will function as your guide more often than the others. His power of truth will serve as the fuel that will fire your desire to learn and grow through the dream worlds. Michael will help you unmask the beliefs that you have accepted as truth in your life. You will be asked to drop self-limiting patterns by re-evaluating your values and your beliefs in order to come to a position of true self-determination.

Days Eight through Twelve: Archangel Raphael

The next five days are led by Raphael, archangel of healing, wholeness, and acceptance. Raphael will help you move from repression of your feelings to the full, honest, and complete expression of your reactions to life. Until you allow yourself to unwind your repressions you will be unable to connect to your deeper feeling nature. Raphael will assist you with this by gently nudging you to express your true feelings to yourself and those around you. This will increase the level of communication within your relationships, bringing you closer to those you love, to God, and to yourself.

Days Thirteen through Sixteen: Archangel Gabriel

After Raphael comes Gabriel, archangel of strength, commitment, and persistence. During the next four days this powerful archangel will lead you to a state of empowerment from which you can define and carry out your life's mission. Gabriel's primary angelic power of acting (i.e., taking action) will help you create change in your life, propelling you toward the achievement of your goals. Gabriel is also the consummate messenger of God. When the Lord has a message of importance to communicate to us on the earth worlds, Archangel Gabriel is usually chosen to deliver it. During your time with Gabriel you may well find that he has a special message for you—direct from the Creator!

Days Seventeen through Twenty: Archangel Uriel

Uriel, the archangel of love, beauty, and awareness, will lead you for the next four nights. He is responsible for teaching us the power of "being." As you study with Uriel, you will learn to appreciate and honor the gift of life that the Creator has given to each of us. Uriel's presence urges us to "stop and smell the roses" even as we are busy engaging life through the powers and process of each of the other archangels.

Days Twenty through Thirty: Advanced Dream Topics

Upon completing the first twenty days of your journey, you will be ready to move on to ten days of advanced dream study. During this time your guiding angel for each night will alternate between the four archangels. This advanced dream study includes such diverse topics as: contacting your deceased loved ones in the dream worlds, meeting your spirit guides, dreaming of past lives, and visiting the heavenly realms.

Skipping and Repeating Dream Journey Days

We've just explained the basic flow and structure of the thirty-day dream program. Your dream journey is designed to provide you with a cumulative learning experience under the tutelage of the four archangels. However, you may wish to change this design to fit your personal preferences. For example, there may be some topics that you do not feel comfortable exploring or that simply do not "resonate" within you. This is perfectly fine. You may skip over these days if you so desire. If you do choose to skip over certain days, we recommend that you take some time to examine why you chose to do so. Perhaps there is an issue that you are afraid to face. We can learn much from our feelings when we choose to consciously explore the motivations that lie hidden beneath them.

Sometimes it may take you more than one night to have the dream experience you desire. In this case feel free to practice a particular dream technique several nights in a row until you are ready to move on.

A Typical Dream Session

Each night's dream session consists of three main parts.

Part One: Tonight's Theme

We start out each session by offering a few pages of material on the evening's dream theme. This information will help prepare you for dream world exploration by focusing your attention on a specific facet of the dream worlds.

Part Two: Attuning Your Consciousness to the Guiding Angel

This section, which consists of prayer and contemplation, prepares your consciousness to connect with your soul self and the angels. The shift in consciousness that this brings will lift and align your energy, thus increasing your ability to receive and understand the wisdom presented to you in the dream worlds.

Prayer of Invocation

To bring you closer to the energy stream of the evening's guiding archangel, you'll recite a special prayer of invocation. By reciting this prayer you issue an invitation to the guiding Archangel to lead you in your dream world study.

Contemplation Period

After reciting the invocation you'll spend a few minutes contemplating a special quote from the guiding archangel. The object of the contemplation period is to further attune yourself to the vibrational field of the guiding angel for the night (similar to tuning into a radio frequency).

Part Three: Tonight's Exercise

Each evening you'll perform a specially designed dream technique. The technique will act as a springboard to take you into the dream worlds where you'll gain deeper insights related to the dream topic for the evening. Upon awakening you'll record your dream experiences in your journal, including as much detail of your dreams and dream fragments as time permits. Using the interpretation guidelines from chapter 3 you will then unseal the hidden messages within your dreams.

We'd like to take a moment to stress that any messages you receive from the angelic realms will always be supportive and loving. Messages that are destructive, violent, or make you feel uncomfortable do not come from the angels. Rather, they usually represent a lost part of you, perhaps an angry or hurt aspect of yourself that wants to express itself within the dream worlds. Destructive messages within your dreams usually occur when the conscious self is in denial or is ashamed of a particular feeling, tendency, or situation. The dream worlds provide a safe environment to explore, express, and heal these feelings.

Beginning Your Journey

And now the time has come to begin your journey. You will start with day 1, "The White Light of God," and end with day 30, "Visiting Heaven." On the way you'll have many opportunities to look forward to—you'll meet with the holy angels of God in their glorious light bodies; you'll connect with the different parts of yourself; and you'll gain an awareness of what you need to do in order to fulfill your part in the divine plan.

May you find success and adventure as you work with the archangels to unseal the hidden messages within your dreams.

> For God speaketh once, yea twice, yet man perceiveth it not.
> In a dream, in a vision of the night, when deep sleep falleth
> upon men, in slumberings upon the bed; Then he openeth the
> ears of men, and sealeth their instruction.
>
> —JOB 33:14–16

The White Light of God

Tonight you will learn about the nature of God and how you can invoke His loving, protective energy during your dream world explorations. We offer this information on the first day of your journey so that you can invoke God's protective energy on all thirty days if you so desire. We will also explore the phenomena of nightmares/invasive dreams and how the white light of God can protect you from these disturbing experiences.

The white light of God, a powerful, protective force, strengthens and cleanses the field of energy that surrounds you (your aura). You can invoke it any time, day or night, when you feel vulnerable or when you simply want to be strengthened and fortified by God's pure light. It is especially helpful for those who experience recurrent nightmares or invasive dreams or for those who simply wish to feel more secure during their nightly dream journeys.

Most of us have had the experience of waking up from a disturbing or frightening dream, typically called a nightmare. Nightmares are dreams that demand our attention in a dramatic and frightening way. They carry urgent messages about personal issues that need to be examined and dealt with—immediately. They are often cries for help from a deeply repressed part of our being. This repressed part of ourselves may represent a characteristic that we are deeply ashamed of having. In fact, we might be in total *conscious* denial that we even possess this characteristic. For example, few of us consciously admit that we are controlling of others.

Although frightening, nightmares are actually the voice of our own subconscious, urging us to take steps toward health and wholeness. A nightmare will often recur or reshape itself nightly until we choose to pay attention to it. It keeps recurring as it tries to find a symbolism that expresses the core issue within that needs deep healing. Oftentimes our nightmares reflect our deepest fears.

Similar to your body's natural defense mechanisms, nightmares can serve as pressure relief valves for unconscious fears. They are ultimately intended to help you rather than harm you. The best way to prevent recurring nightmares is to deal with the core issues that they bring to your attention. Dealing with core issues is not something that can be done overnight, however. It is a process, and it often involves counseling with a trained therapist.

But there *are* several things you can do now to prevent the recurrence of frightening nightmares. The first is to commit to studying your dreams. When you do, your inner dream maker will quickly realize that it no longer has to "scream" at you via nightmares to get your attention.

The second thing you can do to prevent nightmares from recurring is to perform the white light of God technique that we detail for you later in this session. By invoking the light of God, you send a message to your dream maker—a message that lets your dream maker know that you want clearer, less frightening dreams. When you are bathed in the white light of God, your dreams will shape themselves into clear stories that will be easier for you to interpret and less frightening in content.

Your attention to the issues being brought up in your dreams empowers your dream maker to spin *constructive yet pleasant* dreams for you—dreams geared to help you understand your fears and traumas as well as unravel any self-destructive patterns you may have developed in response to these fears.

Invasive Dreams

Occasionally we have dreams in which we feel spiritually assaulted in some way. These dreams are known as invasive dreams, and they differ from nightmares in several ways.

First, in an invasive dream you are lucid about your situation. You know that you are battling a spiritual assault and not an assault to your physical body. Second, you are aware within the invasive dream that you can call upon beings of light for assistance. In a nightmare we are unaware of this—instead of calling for help, we tend to wake up just when the monster is about to catch us.

Invasive dreams can be viewed in two ways: as an actual spiritual attack during the dream state by some foreign, negative entity that wishes to possess you or manipulate your energy in some way; or as an experience in which your negative thought forms (or the negative thought forms of those around you) coalesce into an entity that spiritually attacks you in your dreams.

In either case, we are most susceptible to this type of attack when we feel lonely, hopeless, or sad about something that has happened in our waking life. Invasive dreams are also more likely to occur when we are physically ill or emotionally drained from some life experience. Illness, depression, feeling isolated, and so on, can cause our aura to weaken, thus opening the door to invading entities or negative spirits.

However you tend to view this experience (as an actual psychic attack by a foreign entity or as an attack by your own negative thought forms), invasive dreams cause you to feel as if your very soul is in jeopardy. Our sleep and dream time is sacred. We should feel safe and protected during this vulnerable state.

Invasive Dream Example

The following illustrates an invasive experience and how the angels can help us in the dream state.

PROTECTED BY AN ANGEL

I dreamed I was at a huge gathering of spiritual seekers. It seemed to be a banquet of some kind. I recognized several people, including a lovely and kind woman named Marian. I left the banquet for a few minutes. As I headed outside I suddenly found myself beset by some type of negative spirits or demons.

I was battling them for my life—for my very soul. They kept trying to overcome me—to get close to me; it felt as if they wanted to take over and possess my spirit. I was extremely tired, but I did not give up. Then, just as I yelled at them, "Get away from me, you legions from hell," we all started floating into the air, at least 50 feet above the earth. I saw that we were all dressed in flowing robes, and that the negative spirits were still trying to get close to me. Again I yelled at them, and they backed off a few feet.

I was desperate for help. I could see the crowd below me at the banquet, and I knew they couldn't help me. Almost at the end of my energy, I called out, "Angel, where are you? I need your help."

To my left another being suddenly appeared, arrayed in flowing robes. This being said, "Don't be afraid, for I am an angel—see, I can touch you," he then gently touched me on my arm, "and they cannot."

I understood that the negative spirits could not touch me because I was holding them off—not allowing anything negative to pierce my aura. Even though the negative spirits were beautiful to look upon, I knew that their intentions were not good and that they wanted to suck my energy—to possess me.

The angel's appearance fortified me and gave me strength. The crisis passed, and I flew back down to the banquet to rejoin my friends.

Tonight's exercise contains a technique you can use to protect yourself from this type of invasive dream. In addition to using this technique, you may want to keep several amethyst crystals next to your bed. The energy field that surrounds them enhances dream recall, strengthens the aura, and contains properties of spiritual protection. Put an amethyst crystal under your bed and another on your nightstand.

Attuning Your Consciousness to the Guiding Angel

Michael, chief of the archangels, will be your guide tonight during your journey into the dream worlds. Before performing tonight's dream exercise, use the following invocation and contemplation to attune yourself to his holy presence.

Invocation to Archangel Michael

> *Michael, holy angel of God,*
> *I invite you into my dream worlds and into my consciousness.*
> *I seek to uncover and understand the truth of my choices and to*
> *accept the results of all that I have put into action. Please help*
> *me to see myself more clearly and lend me the wisdom of your*
> *words and presence as I move to lift the Chalice of Justice and to*
> *wield the Sword of Truth. Amen.*

Allow yourself to feel Michael's presence enter your heart. Next, to further attune your consciousness to the guiding presence for tonight, read and contemplate the following words.

> God is the pure energy that vibrates in your soul, that
> pulses within you with each beat of your heart, that builds and
> transmutes worlds, forms, and substances.
>
> —ARCHANGEL MICHAEL

Allow these words to wash over you. Rest with them for a few minutes and feel your whole being come into alignment with their truth. Do this for a few minutes. You have now opened a conduit to the wisdom radiating from the author of tonight's contemplation—Archangel Michael. Open your eyes and continue tonight's session by performing the following dream exercise.

Tonight's Exercise: The White Light of God

As explained earlier, the white light of God technique is a spiritual exercise that strengthens and cleanses your auric field. This technique is very simple.

You can use it to protect and uplift yourself anytime you feel vulnerable, either during the day to seal your aura from negative influences or at night to protect yourself from invasive dreams. By using this technique you also signal your dream maker to send you constructive yet pleasant dreams rather than nightmares. You may wish to tape record this technique so that you can listen to the instructions rather than having to read and memorize them.

1. Light a white candle to symbolize the purity of God's love for you.

2. Close your eyes. Imagine the pure, white, radiant light of God. This beautiful and loving light flows toward you from the heavens.

3. See the radiant white light of God envelop your body from the top of your head to the tips of your toes. Your entire body is surrounded and enfolded in the pure white light of God. Nothing harmful can penetrate this light. You are completely safe, held in the arms of God.

4. Now see this white light extend beyond your body. It flows outward all around you, encircling first your room and then your entire home. This aura of protection extends even beyond your home, out into the neighborhood. It now encompasses the whole area in which you live.

5. See the white light of God continue to expand; your whole country is encompassed within its embrace. Next, you see that the whole world is encircled within this beautiful white light.

6. Know that you are safe and that your loved ones are safe, surrounded in the pure white light of God. Look closely at the light surrounding the earth. Within it you can see beautiful forms flowing in and out, flowing first toward the heavens and then toward the earth. These are the holy angels of God, here to protect you and to bring you messages from God above. They will guard and protect you tonight and every night.

7. Sleep now, content in the knowledge that you are safe in the center of God's white light. Relax and know that the angels of God watch over you and protect you from all negativity while you sleep.

8. As you drift off to sleep and enter the dream worlds, say the following words to yourself:

I am totally safe within the pure white light of God.
Angels surround and protect me, night and day.

Upon awakening in the morning, remember to lie still and keep your eyes closed. Focus your attention on accessing your dream memories. Take some time to allow your dream memories to impress themselves upon your waking mind. After a few minutes, record your dreams in your journal.

When you have finished, begin to unseal the messages hidden within your dreams. Call upon Archangel Michael to bring you insight as you interpret your dreams by saying the following prayer of invocation.

> *Dear Archangel Michael,*
> *Please shine your light of truth upon my dream messages.*
> *Help me to unseal their wisdom so that I might better under-*
> *stand myself, my relationships, and my mission for this lifetime.*
> *Amen.*

Next, perform all seven steps of the interpretation process. The seven steps (from chapter 3) are repeated for you below:

1. Make an inventory or list of each of the characters that appear in your dream, both human and nonhuman.
2. Examine your feelings about the dream characters.
3. Examine your role in the dream and your relationships to the dream characters.
4. Review the actions taking place in the dream.
5. Find out what aspect of yourself the dream characters represent by engaging them in imaginary conversation.
6. Analyze the dream setting (location/time of day/environment).
7. Consider your current life situation.

You will know that you have arrived at the correct dream interpretation when you feel something "click" within you. Don't be discouraged if this doesn't happen right away. The message of your dream may become unsealed over the course of the day or it may take even more time to emerge as you work through your spiritual growth issues.

The Dream Mirror

Tonight's theme is the dream mirror. You will learn about your dream mirror and how it promotes inner healing by reflecting back to you the many different aspects of your character. Tonight's technique will show you how to start building your own personal library of dream symbols and images. We present this information to you early in your thirty-day dream journey so that you can begin the process of building your dream library immediately.

There are no meaningless dreams. All dreams—even partial dreams and dream fragments—contain healing messages. Dreams typically reflect back to us some aspect of our psyche that needs recognition and/or adjustment by the conscious self. This healing function of our dream worlds is always in operation—even when we get so wrapped up in our daily lives that we completely ignore it. During frantically busy times our dream maker typically responds to our lack of attention by spinning bizarre, disconnected, or even silly dreams. Overburdened, we tend to dismiss our wild dreams as meaningless or ridiculous. In reality, our dream maker is trying to use humor and bizarre symbolism to gently capture our attention (rather than sending a nightmare, which demands our attention). It is reminding us of the need to process our life experiences, to slow down, and to take care of ourselves.

Absurd, bizarre, or silly dreams come from your creative subconscious. They usually contain messages about a relationship or a health issue. A good example of this is the "restroom" dream. In this common dream we find ourselves needing to use the toilet but unable to get to a restroom without a great deal of trouble. If we do finally find one, we are unable to use the toilet because it is too dirty, or it is out of order, or it turns out to be a restroom for the opposite sex.

This very frustrating dream appears silly and meaningless on the surface. However, when examined closely, it contains great symbolism. Often it signifies a health concern, such as the need for cleansing—physical, mental, or emotional. Perhaps you are dehydrated and need to drink more water to cleanse your system of toxins. Or perhaps you need to "rid" yourself of a pattern of thinking or habit that no longer serves you. It may also indicate an emotional pattern or response that needs to be examined and released (i.e., flushed).

Sometimes a dream seems meaningless just because we don't understand its symbolism, and so we give up without ever trying to interpret it. Know this—every dream has a purpose, and every dream can be understood and properly interpreted. All we need are the proper dream tools, a willingness to learn, and a commitment to uncovering our personal dream language. Indeed, our dreams are knocking on the door of our consciousness, ripe with insights distilled from our subconscious and our higher self.

Our dreams can shed light on our problems. They help us to understand our personality, our tendencies, and our habits. Armed with this self-knowledge, we can initiate change within ourselves and within our world. The more we listen to our dreams, the more they will reveal to us. Given enough attention, they not only tell us where change is needed, but they also give us clues and direction as to how to accomplish that change.

This healing function of dreams can actually take us several steps beyond the integration of our psyche and the physical health of our body. The closer we get to wholeness and integration, the more our dreams reflect back to us the vast potential of our own creative power. In essence, healing helps us become pure creative beings—the state that our Creator God originally intended for us.

You will find regular use of the following dream mirror technique valuable for several reasons. First, frequent practice of this technique greatly improves the quantity and quality of your dream recall. Second, each nightly expansion of your dream vocabulary creates a fuller picture of the core issues within you that require healing and attention. Last, regular practice of this technique will provide the building blocks (symbols + core issues + personality dynamics) that you will use to create your personal dream symbols library.

Attuning Your Consciousness to the Guiding Angel

Uriel, archangel of love, beauty, and awareness, will be your guide tonight during your journey into the dream worlds. Before performing tonight's dream exercise, use the following invocation and contemplation to attune yourself to his holy presence.

Invocation to Archangel Uriel

> Uriel, holy angel of God,
>> Come to me tonight. May your peaceful presence lead me to a
>> deeper appreciation of my dream worlds. Help me to understand

*and integrate all parts of myself so that I may live a life rooted
in love and joy once again. Let my decisions be based on love,
not fear; and let my every action contribute to the never-ending
demonstration of the Creator's love for all life. Amen.*

Allow yourself to feel Uriel's presence enter your heart. Next, to further
attune your consciousness to the guiding presence for tonight, read and contemplate the following words.

> Those who seek the secrets of life need look no farther
> than themselves. Within each of you lies the complete imprint
> and therefore a trail to the source and beginning of your very
> existence.
>
> —ARCHANGEL URIEL

Allow these words to wash over you. Rest with them for a few minutes and
feel your whole being come into alignment with their truth. Do this for a few
minutes. You have now opened a conduit to the wisdom radiating from the
author of tonight's contemplation—Archangel Uriel. Open your eyes and
continue tonight's session by performing the following dream exercise.

Tonight's Exercise: The Dream Mirror Technique

Sometimes we wake up with only disconnected images from our dreams,
which do not seem to create a story that makes sense. This is when the dream
mirror technique can be especially helpful.

1. Gather a set of blank three-by-five-inch cards and colored pencils or
   markers; place them on a nightstand beside your bed.
2. Before you fall asleep repeat the following affirmation to yourself several times. Remember to create a strong desire within yourself as you
   repeat each word.

   My dreams are healing me.

3. When you awake from a dream, turn on the flashlight that you keep
   beside your bed. Take one of the three-by-five cards and draw a picture
   of one of the images from your dream. Don't worry about your technique. Your purpose is simply to record the symbol. Use a separate card
   for each additional image you recall, no matter how vague or incom-
   plete it might seem.

Drawing pictures of your dream symbols will stimulate better dream recall as well as build a library of your own personal dream symbols and characters.

For example, Linda recently dreamed of someone from her past offering her a wildflower. She did not have complete dream recall, so in this case Linda simply drew a picture of the wildflower on a card and wrote the words *past offering* underneath it. She then took another card and drew a picture of the person who made this offering. She now has two new dream elements to use as she interprets her dreams each night.

You can add color or any other details you might remember at any time to these cards. As you pay attention to your dreams for several weeks, you will begin to see these same symbols recur. They have something to teach you. Each time you dream of them, you will remember new details that you can add to your cards. Soon you will have enough details and enough cards available to determine the meaning of a particular symbol when it occurs in your dreams.

This is the beginning of your dream library of images and symbols. They are unique to you and constitute part of your personal dream language.

———————

Upon awakening in the morning, remember to lie still and keep your eyes closed. Focus your attention on accessing your dream memories. Take some time to allow your dream memories to impress themselves upon your waking mind. After a few minutes, record your dreams in your journal.

When you have finished, begin to unseal the messages hidden within your dreams. Call upon Archangel Uriel to bring you insight as you interpret your dreams by saying the following prayer of invocation.

Dear Archangel Uriel,
  Be with me now as I uncover the hidden meaning of my
dreams. I invoke your joyful and loving presence. Help me see
and appreciate all the parts of myself that I meet within my
dreams. Amen.

Next, perform all seven steps of the interpretation process. The seven steps (from chapter 3) are repeated for you below:

1. Make an inventory or list of each of the characters that appear in your dream, both human and nonhuman.

2. Examine your feelings about the dream characters.

3. Examine your role in the dream and your relationships to the dream characters.

4. Review the actions taking place in the dream.

5. Find out what aspect of yourself the dream characters represent by engaging them in imaginary conversation.

6. Analyze the dream setting (location/time of day/environment).

7. Consider your current life situation.

You will know that you have arrived at the correct dream interpretation when you feel something "click" within you. Don't be discouraged if this doesn't happen right away. The message of your dream may become unsealed over the course of the day or it may take even more time to emerge as you work through your spiritual growth issues.

Meeting Archangel Michael

The theme for tonight is meeting Archangel Michael in your dream worlds. Tonight's information will help you to visualize this glorious angel, whose name means "who is like God." Focusing on Michael will help you hone your powers of discernment. This will bring clarity to your waking-world situations and provide you with penetrating dream interpretation skills.

Known as the angel of protection, Michael carries both the Sword of Truth and the Chalice of Justice. Michael is normally pictured in armor with a sword in his right hand and a scale or chalice in his left hand. Sometimes he is pictured in battle with his heel on the nape of a fallen angel's neck. This symbolizes the ultimate victory of the higher self over the egocentric self.

Saint Michael serves as the cornerstone of the four archangels. Through contact with the energy stream distributed by Michael, we come to see the difference between truth and belief. This new sight will help us to continue the process of manifesting the integrated human being.

Michael helps us to become aware that we have been conditioned by our choices and our experiences. He then helps us focus on how we can change our belief systems in order to have different experiences. His purpose therefore is to bring an understanding of our conditioning and particular set of beliefs to the forefront of our awareness so that we may view the truth of our choices and accept the justice of the energy streams put into motion by our actions. Michael's attributes are truth, honesty, and justice. His process is understanding, and his power is seeing.

Michael's Dream Message

The following text comes from a channeling of Archangel Michael on the topic of dreams.

> Invite me into your dreams and I will shield you with the power
> of your inner truth. I will help you to see and then understand
> your unique composition and lead you to a point of self-power

and self-determination. There are those that speak in my name, but until you meet me in the inner sanctuary of your heart I will forever be only an image and not a spirit-filled reality within your life.

Within dreams you will find it easier to connect to my energy. I will then impart the command of the Lord as it pertains to the complete and honest expression of the life force through your chosen and soul-fashioned personality. Call me and I will appear... In the truth of our Lord.

—MICHAEL

Attuning Your Consciousness to the Guiding Angel

Michael, chief of the archangels, will be your guide tonight during your journey into the dream worlds. Before performing tonight's dream exercise, use the following invocation and contemplation to attune yourself to his holy presence.

Invocation to Archangel Michael

Michael, holy angel of God,
I invite you into my dream worlds and into my consciousness.
I seek to uncover and understand the truth of my choices and to
accept the results of all that I have put into action. Please help
me to see myself more clearly; lend me the wisdom of your words
and presence as I move to lift the Chalice of Justice and wield
the Sword of Truth. Amen.

Allow yourself to feel Michael's presence enter your heart. Next, to further attune your consciousness to the guiding presence for tonight, read and contemplate the following words.

We come as beings of light in your dreams, in your consciousness, and in your heart. As you meditate, meditate upon each of us.

—ARCHANGEL MICHAEL

Allow these words to wash over you. Rest with them for a few minutes and feel your whole being come into alignment with their truth. Do this for a few minutes. You have now opened a conduit to the wisdom radiating from the author of tonight's contemplation—Archangel Michael. Open your eyes and continue tonight's session by performing the following dream exercise.

Tonight's Exercise: Meeting Archangel Michael

Archangel Michael, the archangel of truth, honesty, and justice, wishes to meet with you in your dream worlds tonight. When we meet Michael, we must drop our masks and face our truth. To help set the tone for meeting Michael, relax and repeat the following affirmation before retiring.

> **In my heart I know the truth of myself. I am ready to reveal the truth of myself to the holy Archangel Michael and receive his guidance in my dreams tonight.**

As you repeat this affirmation, feel the presence of Archangel Michael growing stronger and closer. Continue to repeat the affirmation and gently relax into a deep and restful sleep, knowing that you will meet the personage or some aspect of the glorious archangel of God, Michael, in your dreams tonight.

Upon awakening in the morning, remember to lie still and keep your eyes closed. Focus your attention on accessing your dream memories. Take some time to allow your dream memories to impress themselves upon your waking mind. After a few minutes, record your dreams in your journal.

When you have finished, begin to unseal the messages hidden within your dreams. Call upon Archangel Michael to bring you insight as you interpret your dreams by saying the following prayer of invocation.

> *Dear Archangel Michael,*
> *Please shine your light of truth upon my dream messages.*
> *Help me to unseal their wisdom so that I might better under-*
> *stand myself, my relationships, and my mission for this lifetime.*
> *Amen.*

Next, perform all seven steps of the interpretation process. The seven steps (from chapter 3) are repeated for you below:

1. Make an inventory or list of each of the characters that appear in your dream, both human and nonhuman.
2. Examine your feelings about the dream characters.

3. Examine your role in the dream and your relationships to the dream characters.

4. Review the actions taking place in the dream.

5. Find out what aspect of yourself the dream characters represent by engaging them in imaginary conversation.

6. Analyze the dream setting (location/time of day/environment).

7. Consider your current life situation.

You will know that you have arrived at the correct dream interpretation when you feel something "click" within you. Don't be discouraged if this doesn't happen right away. The message of your dream may become unsealed over the course of the day or it may take even more time to emerge as you work through your spiritual growth issues.

Dream of Truth

Now that you have met with Archangel Michael in the dream worlds, you are ready to explore his main virtue: truth. Cultivating the virtue of truth in your world is critical to living a life of balance and inner peace. Of the various aspects of truth that exist, Michael teaches that the most important is self-truth—being honest with ourselves about our feelings and our thoughts. Tonight we will review the importance of honoring the truth that exists within each part of the self.

Dreams contain encoded messages from the different parts of the self: the soul self, the higher self, the conscious self, the emotional self, and the subconscious self. Each part is continually trying to communicate with you—to bring to your conscious awareness all the lost, repressed, and hurting parts of yourself.

When your conscious mind acknowledges and examines its repressed pain, it has initiated the healing process of integrating these lost parts and making you whole. During this process you will uncover your self-limiting patterns. You can then make the conscious choice to release them. By releasing your self-limiting patterns you will be able to connect more clearly to your soul—the part of you that contains the blueprint for your growth and expansion in this lifetime.

The following example illustrates the importance of communicating with the parts of your self. Without clear communication (i.e., understanding their messages) you will be unable to integrate their wisdom into your life. This limits your ability to project the complete truth of yourself into the world around you.

Imagine a family consisting of a mother, a father, and a child. Next, imagine that the family members have just arrived at a counseling center. They are having problems communicating. Among other things, the mother and father argue over different ways to discipline the child.

Lacking the tools or training to communicate lovingly and effectively, the mother and father have hurt each other. They have hidden their feelings from themselves and from each other, resulting in a state of repression. This has created barriers, not only between them but within their hearts as well. The child, sensing the inner pressure and conflict between the parents, has begun to act out the patterns that he has observed and learned. A drama has ensued that consumes the family in a round-robin of miscommunication. Without the proper care and attention, this cycle will probably lead to further choices based on repression rather than honest expression.

Our imaginary family is fortunate. They at least have the awareness to realize they have a problem that needs handling. The parents know that something feels wrong. They may feel guilty or, more likely, they may think that their spouse is not seeing something clearly. They may try to convince themselves that the problem does not exist within themselves. The parents may even blame the child's actions as causing the tensions they feel.

In any case, our make-believe family has chosen to address the confusing and distressing state they have found themselves in. They need to learn how to communicate with each other in a healthy manner. They can assist one another and enhance their life together by providing the basic human needs that their roles define. Beneath their pain, arguing, and fear of rejection lives the human desire for acceptance—to give and to receive love.

The counselor begins by listening to each of the members of this family as they voice their concerns and begin to express themselves in honesty to each other (and perhaps to themselves!). His initial goal is to help them feel comfortable enough with themselves and safe enough with each other so they can identify and express their true feelings. Without getting beyond the barrier of their repressed reef of fears, true and lasting communication cannot occur. Decisions made unconsciously or from inaccurate information will usually just lead to more confusion and misdirected actions in the future.

Consider our family as a closed loop with a certain amount of energy that is continually being transferred from one person to another. As one person relieves pressure by bursting out in anger rather than expressing hurt in a constructive way, the other members are compelled by that energy to react, often in a conditioned pattern that they learned as young children, trying to survive.

In order to help these people communicate better, the counselor may present information and examples from others' situations and experiences. Eventually, if the family commits to the process of therapy, each member will find relief. The child, seeing the parents relate better as role models, will start to change his patterns. And the parents, equipped with better methods for interpreting their own feelings and using words and actions to communicate them clearly, will begin to open up their hearts once again.

The above example illustrates the situation that we and our self-segments (the soul, higher conscious, emotional, and subconscious selves) face in our day-to-day life. Extending this analogy a step farther, we find that the father represents our conscious self-segment, the self that believes it is in control of the choices that it makes. The mother represents the nurturing emotional self-segment that is trying to work for expression amid the strong currents of opposing needs. And the child represents the subconscious/basic self that presents its needs in symbols that are sometimes very hard to decipher, making it difficult to find the hidden causes for its reactions, actions, and messages.

Who does the family counselor represent? The counselor represents the soul self; the self that is in direct contact with the spirit and God worlds. The soul self has spun the personality into existence in the material worlds. The personality is like a pair of colored glasses through which everything we view in the world is modified. Its purpose is to move us into specific areas of experience as desired by the soul self. The soul knows its purpose for this lifetime—the mission that it wishes to accomplish. It counsels and works with the other self-segments. When the self-segments realize the importance of co-communication with one another, the soul is present to lead and teach.

The act of the fictional family going to the counseling center represents the act of the an individual like yourself choosing to look at your dream worlds for clarity and understanding of the human experience, not only in a dream state but also in the waking state, each and every day of your life. The stories and illustrations that the counselor used to help this family represent the wisdom accessed from the self-segment known as the higher self.

The preceding story provides us with an example of the process of integration. It exemplifies how we can benefit when all our self-segments come into an honest and truthful understanding of one another. This understanding relieves pressure and diffuses the need to act out potentially destructive urges.

The dream worlds offer a natural environment to discern the truth of our own inner thoughts and feelings. Using the light of the soul self and the focus of the conscious self we can uncover and begin to understand the mysterious ways that we communicate with ourselves in our dreams.

Attuning Your Consciousness to the Guiding Angel

Michael, chief of the archangels, will be your guide tonight during your journey into the dream worlds. Before performing tonight's dream exercise, use the following invocation and contemplation to attune yourself to his holy presence.

Invocation to Archangel Michael

Michael, holy angel of God,
    I invite you into my dream worlds and into my consciousness.
I seek to uncover and understand the truth of my choices and to
accept the results of all that I have put into action. Please help
me to see myself more clearly and lend me the wisdom of your
words and presence as I move to lift the Chalice of Justice and to
wield the Sword of Truth. Amen.

Allow yourself to feel Michael's presence enter your heart. Next, to further attune your consciousness to the guiding presence for tonight, read and contemplate the following words.

    I come to you to offer you the chalice of purity. As you
    drink of it, you drink of your own truth, accepting and gaining
    nourishment from the inner truth that is you.

—ARCHANGEL MICHAEL

Allow these words to wash over you. Rest with them for a few minutes and feel your whole being come into alignment with their truth. Do this for a few minutes. You have now opened a conduit to the wisdom radiating from the author of tonight's contemplation—Archangel Michael. Open your eyes and continue tonight's session by performing the following dream exercise.

Tonight's Exercise: Dream of Truth

Michael, the archangel of truth, honesty, and justice, will show you an aspect of your life that is out of tune with your inner truth. Like an image seen through a telescope that becomes sharper as you focus, your inner image will become clearer as Michael's energy helps you to focus on your inner truth. During this process you will become aware of the protective masks that you have grown accustomed to wearing. You may also become more aware of the other parts of yourself as they present their truth to you in your dreams.

As you fall asleep tonight, repeat the following prayer to Archangel Michael. It will help set the tone for your dreams.

Dear Archangel Michael,
    I desire to know the truth of myself. I no longer wish to hide
my inner self from the world. Help me to see with clarity and
accept with compassion the complete truth of who I am. Amen.

As you repeat the prayer feel the presence of Archangel Michael growing stronger and closer. Continue to repeat the prayer and gently relax into a deep and restful sleep knowing that tonight you will learn more about the truth of who you are.

———————

Upon awakening in the morning, remember to lie still and keep your eyes closed. Focus your attention on accessing your dream memories. Take some time to allow your dream memories to impress themselves upon your waking mind. After a few minutes, record your dreams in your journal.

When you have finished, begin to unseal the messages hidden within your dreams. Call upon Archangel Michael to bring you insight as you interpret your dreams by saying the following prayer of invocation.

> *Dear Archangel Michael,*
> *Please shine your light of truth upon my dream messages. Help me to unseal their wisdom so that I might better understand myself, my relationships, and my mission for this lifetime. Amen.*

Next, perform all seven steps of the interpretation process. The seven steps (from chapter 3) are repeated for you below:

1. Make an inventory or list of each of the characters that appear in your dream, both human and nonhuman.

2. Examine your feelings about the dream characters.

3. Examine your role in the dream and your relationships to the dream characters.

4. Review the actions taking place in the dream.

5. Find out what aspect of yourself the dream characters represent by engaging them in imaginary conversation.

6. Analyze the dream setting (location/time of day/environment).

7. Consider your current life situation.

You will know that you have arrived at the correct dream interpretation when you feel something "click" within you. Don't be discouraged if this doesn't happen right away. The message of your dream may become unsealed over the course of the day or it may take even more time to emerge as you work through your spiritual growth issues.

Recognizing Your Patterns

Last night you learned about the importance of self-truth. Tonight, Archangel Michael will show you how to apply self-truth to your life in a practical way by helping you to uncover your unconscious patterns—patterns that may be holding you back from achieving your life's purpose.

Michael teaches that recognizing your patterns is crucial in charting your own course in life. Until we can see our own patterns, we are destined to continue in the same direction, unaware that we may be simply following a ritualistic form of living.

Just as a ship's course is affected by the currents that swirl around it, your progress in accomplishing your life's mission is affected by the energy patterns that surround you. If, as the captain of your ship, you do not take into account the direction and energy of the currents, you'll end up miles off course. In the same way, you must take into account the patterns of your life—conscious and unconscious—in order to reach your desired goal.

Learning to recognize your patterns comes through developing discernment. Discernment is the ability to look at your life as if you were outside of your body, looking back at your personal world from an objective viewpoint. This objectivity will help you identify and accept your subconscious patterns. Then, from a position of discernment and awareness, you can change those patterns if you so desire. In this way you become the true master of your own destiny.

You can increase your powers of discernment in several ways. One way is to practice shifting your attention from processing information through the physical senses to processing information through the spiritual senses. This task is not an easy undertaking because our conditioned patterns tend to lock us into the human state. Not being aware that we are controlled by our conditioned patterns, how can we hope to break those patterns? How can we change and freely choose future cycles of experience?

The best and perhaps only way to break a pattern (our conditioned responses to stimuli) is to bring another energy source to bear upon it.

Whether the energy comes from spiritual power, emotional release, or some other event makes no difference. It is always another source of energy that comes into play. We can respond to the introduction of this new energy source in a variety of ways: We can ignore and repel it; view and discard it; or view, integrate, and take action upon it. The latter option creates change and fosters growth.

For example, imagine that you have fallen into the habit of oversleeping. Each morning you get up ten minutes later than you should. As a result, you get to work ten to fifteen minutes late each day. You are surprised that no one at work mentions your tardiness. Your co-workers and your supervisor ignore it completely. Days go by, and then weeks pass as your pattern becomes more and more ingrained. Then an unexpected change occurs at work; you find out that you have a new supervisor. On her first day, your new supervisor calls you into her office to tell you, in no uncertain terms, that you must get to work on time—or else!

In this example the new energy source is the new supervisor who, unlike her predecessor, has stringent views on tardiness. She made it very clear that she would not tolerate this behavior. It also seems clear that until her energy came into play, you had no incentive to change your pattern.

Rather than wait for another energy source to act upon us, we can take charge of our direction in life by choosing to tap into new energy sources through meditation, prayer, channeling, dream work, or any active focus on personal growth issues. We can then ride these energy sources to greater levels of awareness about our personal patterns. In addition to making us aware of our patterns, these newly tapped energy sources can assist us in changing those patterns.

Often the only way to grow is to let go of old patterns that hold us in repetitive cycles of experience. For example, a woman climbing a ladder would make no upward progress if she did not let go of each rung to grab the one above it. The same holds true for spiritual progress. As we move from one cycle of experience to another, we learn to accept that cycles will come and go. What was once our entire world and belief system becomes a set of memories, stored for later viewing in both joy and sorrow, as we expand our awareness of the reality of life.

Maximizing the Dream World's Benefits by Overcoming Past Patterns

In order to experience more vivid, dynamic dream worlds, we must first learn to trust. If we fear for the safety of our physical self, we will likely have trouble entering a deep sleep state. A state of deep sleep is important because it facilitates the movement of our awareness away from the distractions of the physical worlds. Without the freedom to enter the deeper levels of the dream worlds, we limit both the time spent in the dream worlds and the depth to which our consciousness can penetrate them. This will limit our ability to receive and process the hidden messages from our dream maker.

Achieving a deep level of dream-world immersion requires that we allow our conscious mind to let go of its day-to-day concerns. If you are having trouble doing this during sleep, you may unconsciously be reacting to a past-life engram (memory pattern).

For example, perhaps in a past lifetime you were in charge of protecting your platoon, but you inadvertently fell asleep while on night watch, thus contributing to a disaster. The emotional imprint of this highly charged experience then becomes part of the residue that you carry from lifetime to lifetime. This sort of residue from the past can cause insomnia as well as other types of sleep disorders. Because such life-altering patterns come from the distant past they are difficult to recognize, let alone overcome.

To better overcome engrams, we suggest that you practice the art of forgiving yourself. Forgiveness is a deep and ongoing process that consists of accepting what we have done in the past and making a commitment toward positive change in the future. Prayer can be an effective tool in the healing process of forgiveness.

You can also overcome your engrams by working consciously with the four archangels. They can help you to explore your past life experiences while in the dream state or during your daily meditations. The complete processing of past experiences will help remove engrams. This is critical in achieving deep and effective dream world exploration.

Attuning Your Consciousness to the Guiding Angel

Michael, chief of the archangels, will be your guide tonight during your journey into the dream worlds. Before performing tonight's dream exercise, use the following invocation and contemplation to attune yourself to his holy presence.

Invocation to Archangel Michael

> *Michael, holy angel of God,*
> *I invite you into my dream worlds and into my consciousness.*
> *I seek to uncover and understand the truth of my choices and to*
> *accept the results of all that I have put into action. Please help*
> *me to see myself more clearly and lend me the wisdom of your*
> *words and presence as I move to lift the Chalice of Justice and*
> *wield the Sword of Truth. Amen.*

Allow yourself to feel Michael's presence enter your heart. Next, to further attune your consciousness to the guiding presence for tonight, read and contemplate the following words.

> By using the harmonics of honesty to allow your higher
> self to shine above you and through you, you will bring peace
> into manifestation, and your choices will be made from clarity
> rather than through dysfunction.
>
> —ARCHANGEL MICHAEL

Allow these words to wash over you. Rest with them for a few minutes and feel your whole being come into alignment with their truth. Do this for a few minutes. You have now opened a conduit to the wisdom radiating from the author of tonight's contemplation—Archangel Michael. Open your eyes and continue tonight's session by performing the following dream exercise.

Tonight's Exercise: Recognizing Your Patterns

Tonight's dream focus is with Archangel Michael, who helps us to see our conditioned patterns—patterns that can cause us to repeat similar experiences again and again. Michael also helps us to understand how our beliefs have been formed. He separates the concepts of truth and belief so that we can see how we have fashioned our lives.

Your dream worlds provide a safe place to see your patterns acted out in 3D from an objective viewpoint—something that is harder to do in the waking state. As you go to sleep tonight say the following prayer to Archangel Michael several times. It will help set the tone for your night's dreams.

Dear Michael,
> *Come to me in my dreams tonight, holy archangel of God.*
> *Show me the hidden patterns that fashion my earthly experience.*
> *This I ask of you through the universal Christ energy. Amen.*

As you repeat this prayer feel the presence of Archangel Michael growing stronger and closer. Continue to repeat the prayer and gently relax into a deep and restful sleep, knowing that soon your dreams will highlight one or more patterns that you need to resolve in some way.

Upon awakening in the morning, remember to lie still and keep your eyes closed. Focus your attention on accessing your dream memories. Take some time to allow your dream memories to impress themselves upon your waking mind. After a few minutes, record your dreams in your journal.

When you have finished, begin to unseal the messages hidden within your dreams. Call upon Archangel Michael to bring you insight as you interpret your dreams by saying the following prayer of invocation.

> *Dear Archangel Michael,*
> *Please shine your light of truth upon my dream messages.*
> *Help me to unseal their wisdom so that I might better under-*
> *stand myself, my relationships, and my mission for this lifetime.*
> *Amen.*

Next, perform all seven steps of the interpretation process. The seven steps (from chapter 3) are repeated for you below:

1. Make an inventory or list of each of the characters that appear in your dream, both human and nonhuman.
2. Examine your feelings about the dream characters.
3. Examine your role in the dream and your relationships to the dream characters.
4. Review the actions taking place in the dream.
5. Find out what aspect of yourself the dream characters represent by engaging them in imaginary conversation.
6. Analyze the dream setting (location/time of day/environment).
7. Consider your current life situation.

You will know that you have arrived at the correct dream interpretation when you feel something "click" within you. Don't be discouraged if this doesn't happen right away. The message of your dream may become unsealed over the course of the day or it may take even more time to emerge as you work through your spiritual growth issues.

DAY 6

Facing Your Fears

We all have fears. What do you fear? The loss of a job, the end of a relationship, or perhaps the final experience of life—death itself? This evening's dream study will help you gain the courage to face such fears.

Facing fears may initially make you uncomfortable, but the process of recognizing, evaluating, and understanding your fears can free you from them. In order to accomplish our life's mission and to reach our full potential we need to first free ourselves of our fears.

To identify our fears, we must resist the instinct to repress our reactions to the events in our life that cause us to feel fear. When we repress our reactions to life, our conscious mind is not in a position to evaluate the underlying causes of our fears. If we fail to evaluate and identify the underlying causes, we will not be able to free ourselves from their negative influences.

Fear can affect the physical body. If we repress our fears, denying that they exist, then the unprocessed energy from this fear can manifest as stress-related health problems. Therefore, processing our emotions is important, for it is in the processing of the experience—good or bad—that we gain the wisdom that lies within as well as relieve the pressure of bottling up our reactions to life.

When we refuse to acknowledge and process our emotions, specifically the emotion of fear, it is as if we ate some food but were unable (unwilling) to digest it. Over a period of time our body would waste away from a lack of nourishment. In much the same way, if we fail to process our emotions, we rob ourselves of the inner wisdom that lies within the experiences of our life, and our spirit would soon wither away into a state of depression and addictive behaviors.

As human beings, we are wrapped up in unexpressed emotional energy that we must unravel or we will be forever bound to our fears. Once you begin to express your fears to yourself, you can then drill down to the emotions that lie beneath. Eventually, through this process, you will reach the core of your being, and a greater degree of peace will enter your life.

Sometimes fear serves a positive purpose, warning us to avoid known dangers that have caused us pain in the past. But when fear freezes us into a state of inaction, we become paralyzed, unable to progress toward our goals or to expand our consciousness into a deeper awareness and knowledge of life. Paralyzing fears are the most difficult fears to face, but you must face them head-on. Be brave and seize the opportunity to deal with your fear by acknowledging and accepting it. Don't ignore the experience and stuff its energy within your unconscious self.

Caution-based fears, while not as debilitating as fears that immobilize us, nevertheless can and do affect our lives. The danger in allowing our caution-based fears to continue without examination is that we tend to close ourselves off from whole areas of life. This limits our ability to gain new experiences.

For example, if you went on a blind date and had an awful time (perhaps you were embarrassed or felt rejected), your caution-based fear pattern would influence you to reject such dates in the future. Your fear has altered your future choices and the possible opportunities those choices would present. You may have indefinitely postponed a potential soul-mate meeting by your choice to accept your fear as reality. Remember, even though we can learn from our past experiences, they are not absolute predictors of future events.

The mystery of the future remains just that—a mystery. Like characters in the pages of a novel, we learn of our destiny and experience our life one page at a time. Life is an adventure. Facing our fears can help us to experience all life has to offer.

Michael can help you overcome irrational fears and break through the internal barriers that prevent you from moving beyond your self-limiting fears. He can help you gain the experience you wish in your life. Until you process your fears, they will exert a negative force that impedes your ability to fulfill your life's purpose.

Attuning Your Consciousness to the Guiding Angel

Michael, chief of the archangels, will be your guide tonight during your journey into the dream worlds. Before performing tonight's dream exercise, use the following invocation and contemplation to attune yourself to his holy presence.

Invocation to Archangel Michael

> *Michael, holy angel of God,*
>> *I invite you into my dream worlds and into my consciousness.*
>> *I seek to uncover and understand the truth of my choices and to*
>> *accept the results of all that I have put into action. Please help*

me to see myself more clearly and lend me the wisdom of your
words and presence as I move to lift the Chalice of Justice and
wield the Sword of Truth. Amen.

Allow yourself to feel Michael's presence enter your heart. Next, to further attune your consciousness to the guiding presence for tonight, read and contemplate the following words.

> Deeper and deeper levels of honesty require you to show
> more and more of yourself to yourself and the world. A deeper
> understanding of justice will lead you to accept the cycles of
> experience you have chosen.
>
> —ARCHANGEL MICHAEL

Allow these words to wash over you. Rest with them for a few minutes and feel your whole being come into alignment with their truth. Do this for a few minutes. You have now opened a conduit to the wisdom radiating from the author of tonight's contemplation—Archangel Michael. Open your eyes and continue tonight's session by performing the following dream exercise.

Tonight's Exercise: Facing Your Fears

We all have fears. Some are logical while others border on the irrational (phobias). What do you fear? Michael can help you to identify your fear and face it. You can do this in your dreams tonight. Your dream worlds provide a safe place to process to the root of your fear.

As you go to sleep tonight identify the one event, thing, or person that you feel the most fear about. Next, recite the following prayer several times.

> *Dear Archangel Michael—archangel of truth, honesty, and*
> *justice,*
> *Please help me tonight in my dreams as I attempt to face my*
> *fear of_____ (name your fear). I desire*
> *to understand my fear and its origin. I wish to grow in courage*
> *and honesty daily. This I ask of you through the universal Christ*
> *energy. Amen.*

As you repeat the prayer feel the presence of Archangel Michael growing stronger and closer. Continue to repeat the prayer and gently relax into a deep and restful sleep knowing that soon you will have a dream that exposes a fear that keeps you from taking positive action toward your life's mission.

———————

Upon awakening in the morning, remember to lie still and keep your eyes closed. Focus your attention on accessing your dream memories. Take some time to allow your dream memories to impress themselves upon your waking mind. After a few minutes, record your dreams in your journal.

When you have finished, begin to unseal the messages hidden within your dreams. Call upon Archangel Michael to bring you insight as you interpret your dreams by saying the following prayer of invocation.

> *Dear Archangel Michael,*
>   *Please shine your light of truth upon my dream messages.*
> *Help me to unseal their wisdom so that I might better under-*
> *stand myself, my relationships, and my mission for this lifetime.*
> *Amen.*

Next, perform all seven steps of the interpretation process. The seven steps (from chapter 3) are repeated for you below:

1. Make an inventory or list of each of the characters that appear in your dream, both human and nonhuman.
2. Examine your feelings about the dream characters.
3. Examine your role in the dream and your relationships to the dream characters.
4. Review the actions taking place in the dream.
5. Find out what aspect of yourself the dream characters represent by engaging them in imaginary conversation.
6. Analyze the dream setting (location/time of day/environment).
7. Consider your current life situation.

You will know that you have arrived at the correct dream interpretation when you feel something "click" within you. Don't be discouraged if this doesn't happen right away. The message of your dream may become unsealed over the course of the day or it may take even more time to emerge as you work through your spiritual growth issues.

Conscious Dreaming

Conscious dreaming is, in part, the ability to inject your conscious will into your dream world environment. Tonight we will discuss how to induce a conscious dream and how to identify and create your own conscious dreaming trigger points. We will also address the difficulty in maintaining your awareness once you realize you are consciously dreaming.

The primary purpose of conscious dreaming is to receive and process the messages from our self-segments in full consciousness. Yet conscious dreaming also serves as a laboratory for virtual experimentation. You can visit with deceased loved ones in full consciousness, work on solutions to your day-to-day problems, and resolve relationship tensions. All this occurs in a world without time and space constraints—in your dream worlds.

Desire and Conscious Dreaming

One of most influential factors in achieving the conscious dreaming state is our desire to experience a particular state of being. Desire is an intense and magnetically charged stream of energy whose main purpose is to effectuate an end result—a reorganization of material matter and substance. In dreams, the very strength of our waking desires can inject our conscious mind into the dream experience.

Peter relates a recurring conscious dream from his adolescence.

> When I was about ten years old, my father was elected to a position that required my family and me to move from my childhood home of San Francisco to the tropical paradise of Hawaii. Even though paradise beckoned, I found it very hard to imagine leaving the only friends, school, and relatives I had known all my life. I did not want to leave. In the end we moved to our new home far away from the one where my true heart remained.
>
> Over the course of the next few months, I processed feelings of homesickness for San Francisco. I looked forward to summer

and the chance to return to the mainland to visit. In the meantime, my desire to be with old friends and familiar surroundings grew so strong that it created the following dream experience.

The Homesick Dream

In this dream I stood outside of my grandparents' front door, looking at the doorbell. The focal point of my extended family in San Francisco was my maternal grandparents' home. My mother took my brother and me there quite frequently after school and on weekends since they lived only about ten blocks from us.

Their home was one of the San Francisco–style row houses, pushed up close against its neighbors. Each row house was a two-story home, and each had steps going up to the front door from the sidewalk. I looked back down the steps to the street.

It was early in the morning with an overcast sky. I felt excited to be at my grandparents' home again. I knew that I was in San Francisco, but I had not yet realized I was dreaming. A moment later I was startled into conscious awareness of my situation when I thought, I don't remember flying from Hawaii to San Francisco. In fact, I don't even remember waking up this morning! How did I get here?

At this point the dream would fade and I would either wake up or fall into a dreamless sleep. I had this dream three or four times that year. Each time, I was again excited to find myself back in my home city, and each time I wondered how I got there. Eventually, my conscious mind and my dream self connected. Within the dream I was able to tell myself that I was only dreaming and that my body must be asleep in bed.

Peter's experience illustrates conscious dreaming. It shows how the conscious self can begin to filter into the dream state. In this example, a strong desire was the key motivating factor in the conscious self making a connection with the dream worlds. For Peter, the experience of going back to his home town was so important to him that his conscious self was brought into the dream to experience and question the authenticity of the dream images. Something was "too good to be true," and some part of him questioned the experience in order to prove that it was indeed "real."

A major benefit of conscious dreaming is that while our body sleeps and recharges, we can continue to learn as well as have enlightening adventures.

We can have dreams of fulfillment and reassurance, expand our knowledge base, and gain insights into our daily problems and circumstances. Sometimes a conscious dream experience can invigorate the energy of our physical body. This is what happened for Linda after a conscious dream experience she had several years ago.

SKIING IN THE ALPS

The dream took place in the daytime. The setting was the beautiful Swiss Alps. I skied expertly down a mountain and felt a glorious sense of freedom and exhilaration. After I'd finished that run and was in the process of taking off my skis, I "awoke" within the dream. I knew right away that there was no way I could actually be physically present in the Swiss Alps, yet at the same time I found I could look around and enjoy the beauty of the mountains and the crisp freshness of the air. So I decided to test my dream environment. I reached down and touched the brilliant snow and cold ice. It felt completely real, yet I knew I had not made the trip to Switzerland. I then awoke from my dream. My body felt totally refreshed, energized, and perfectly in tune—just as if I'd actually spent the day on the slopes!

Maintaining Conscious Awareness

The most common problem experienced during conscious dreaming is that of losing your awareness of the dream state. This can come from not achieving a deep enough dream state, or from the excitement of realizing that you are dreaming. Losing your awareness of the dream state normally occurs at the "realization" moment, the moment in which your conscious self awakens within the dream. At this transition point you become aware that you are dreaming.

At this realization time you may also become aware of the position of your physical body. If this occurs, your attention is drawn back to the physical body and the dream world begins to fade away. As the dream world's impact lessens, your contact with the dream breaks, and you will either awaken or lose contact with your conscious self within your dream.

Conscious dreaming can thus be likened to donning a wetsuit and an oxygen tank and diving into unknown waters to experience life in an underwater environment. If you become too aware of your physical self while dreaming, it is as if you have removed your wetsuit and oxygen tank—you must return to the surface immediately.

If you can keep from returning to waking consciousness during a conscious dreaming episode, you will have to contend with a secondary problem: the loss of conscious awareness within the dream state. When this happens, the predominate self-segment responsible for the dream message takes complete control and you fall into a traditional dream experience.

Awakening in the Dream Using Trigger Points

The conscious dreaming state can occur naturally during sleep or it can be self-induced. Peter's dream is an example of a naturally occurring conscious dream, that is, he did not go to sleep intending to travel to San Francisco in his dreams. Luckily for us, there are multiple ways to awaken yourself in the dream state in a more directed manner.

Using what we call trigger points, you can train a level of your conscious awareness to monitor and respond to a certain phrase, symbol, or action while you are dreaming. Peter's trigger point, which he has developed over the years, involves a simple electric light switch. If at any time during a dream Peter turns on a light switch and the light fails to illuminate, Peter's conscious mind is alerted to the fact that he is indeed in the dream worlds.

His trigger point carries with it a semi-shock, much like the physical feeling you experience when you are startled. Fortunately for Peter, the opportunity to consciously dream outweighs the rather unpleasant effect of his specific trigger point.

Do you have trigger points? If you don't, you can start training your mind to awaken within a dream by imagining a particular action, symbol, or phrase and then tying that image to a strong emotionally charged memory. It doesn't need to be frightening or startling, but it must have enough intensity to connect and draw your conscious mind into your dream worlds.

Attuning Your Consciousness to the Guiding Angel

Michael, chief of the archangels, will be your guide tonight during your journey into the dream worlds. Before performing tonight's dream exercise, use the following invocation and contemplation to attune yourself to his holy presence.

Invocation to Archangel Michael

> Michael, holy angel of God,
>   I invite you into my dream worlds and into my consciousness.
> I seek to uncover and understand the truth of my choices and to
> accept the results of all that I have put into action. Please help
> me to see myself more clearly and lend me the wisdom of your

words and presence as I move to lift the Chalice of Justice and wield the Sword of Truth. Amen.

Allow yourself to feel Michael's presence enter your heart. Next, to further attune your consciousness to the guiding presence for tonight, read and contemplate the following words.

> Consciousness consists of the immediate realization of the life force. It is in part an awareness of the environment you exist in at this moment and the worlds you choose to place your attention on at this moment. By changing your attitude you change your destiny.
>
> —ARCHANGEL MICHAEL

Allow these words to wash over you. Rest with them for a few minutes and feel your whole being come into alignment with their truth. Do this for a few minutes. You have now opened a conduit to the wisdom radiating from the author of tonight's contemplation—Archangel Michael. Open your eyes and continue tonight's session by performing the following dream exercise.

Tonight's Exercise: Experiencing Conscious Dreaming

The key to success with this exercise depends upon one main factor: *Your purpose for exploring this phenomenon must be strong enough to generate the energy required to experience it.* In other words, you will have greater success if your reason for pursuing conscious dreaming generates enough passion to move you past the barrier of unconsciousness while in the sleep state.

The following example illustrates the amount of desire you must generate to accomplish conscious dreaming. Imagine, for a moment, what it would be like to be paralyzed and unable to walk or drive a car. How great would your desire be for mobility? For example, in his book, *Still Me,* Christopher Reeve explains that he often dreams of walking, running, and riding horses. He is not restricted in his dreams by his current physical limitations. That same intensity to experience freedom of function must be generated within you if you wish to experience conscious dreaming consistently and with results. Try the following exercise.

1. Choose your dream goal, a situation that you wish to experience in the dream state. Perhaps you'd like to visit a temple in the spiritual worlds, connect with the guidance of the four archangels, or even contact a deceased loved one. Whatever you choose as your dream goal, you

must be confident that you can generate enough intensity of energy in desiring that goal.

2. Prepare for sleep. After you pick your dream goal, make yourself comfortable for bed. Make sure that you have taken care of all your nightly chores. Ensure that all is quiet as you lay down to sleep. Relax and take a few deep breaths. As you do, silently repeat the following affirmation.

> **As I go to sleep tonight I will dream of _____**
> **(state your wish). I will have conscious awareness within**
> **my dreams. I now have the ability to converse in full**
> **conscious awareness with entities and beings,**
> **both living and dead, in my dreams.**

3. Generate desire for the dream goal. After you repeat the affirmation, allow yourself to relax further. As your body continues to relax, begin to generate a strong desire to experience your dream goal(s). One way to do this is to think of all the things that you will gain by achieving your dream goal. Ask yourself how you will benefit from experiencing your dream goal(s). Make sure to imagine how you will feel when you achieve the goal. Make it real by concentrating upon these factors.

   Don't be afraid to be honest with yourself. Remember that it takes courage to look into the mirror of truth. Consider what you will lose if you do not have the experience that you wish in your dream state. How will you suffer from the lack of this experience? Your answers can assist you in generating a strong magnetic field of energy. A field that is strong and powerful enough can pull your conscious mind into your dream environment.

4. Enter the sleep state. You have affirmed your goal and generated a strong energy field for dream awareness. Begin to move into the sleep state while holding an image of your goal in your mind. Release your conscious awareness and allow yourself to slip into a deep and relaxing sleep.

At some point you will find yourself in a dream. You may have conscious awareness at the start of the dream. If not, then at some point during the dream a trigger point will "awaken" you into conscious awareness. Once conscious, you can begin to converse, experiment, and experience with the force of your conscious will. When in this state you can also connect to other personalities, situations, and circumstances. These personalities can be living or dead. They may be friends, relatives, spirit guides, or angels. However, it is important to remember that the personalities you encounter within your dreams can also represent symbols and personality traits that are being presented to you by your other self-segments to promote healing and integration.

Upon awakening in the morning, remember to lie still and keep your eyes closed. Focus your attention on accessing your dream memories. Take some time to allow your dream memories to impress themselves upon your waking mind. After a few minutes, record your dreams in your journal.

When you have finished, begin to unseal the messages hidden within your dreams. Call upon Archangel Michael to bring you insight as you interpret your dreams by saying the following prayer of invocation.

> *Dear Archangel Michael,*
> *Please shine your light of truth upon my dream messages.*
> *Help me to unseal their wisdom so that I might better under-*
> *stand myself, my relationships, and my mission for this lifetime.*
> *Amen.*

Next, perform all seven steps of the interpretation process. The seven steps (from chapter 3) are repeated for you below:

1. Make an inventory or list of each of the characters that appear in your dream, both human and nonhuman.
2. Examine your feelings about the dream characters.
3. Examine your role in the dream and your relationships to the dream characters.
4. Review the actions taking place in the dream.
5. Find out what aspect of yourself the dream characters represent by engaging them in imaginary conversation.
6. Analyze the dream setting (location/time of day/environment).
7. Consider your current life situation.

You will know that you have arrived at the correct dream interpretation when you feel something "click" within you. Don't be discouraged if this doesn't happen right away. The message of your dream may become unsealed over the course of the day or it may take even more time to emerge as you work through your spiritual growth issues.

DAY 8

Embracing Each Part
of Your Self

Up to this point of your journey you have been guided primarily by Archangel Michael. Now it is time to begin working with Archangel Raphael. Tonight Raphael will help you to learn how to embrace each part of your self (your self-segments). These parts are known as the soul self, the higher self, the emotional self, the basic/subconscious self, and the conscious/intellectual self.

As the archangel of healing, wholeness, and acceptance, Raphael will direct you to an understanding of the concerns expressed by your self-segments. His energy will help you to give the different parts of your self permission to freely express themselves. This relieves inner pressure, leads to greater dream clarity, and facilitates efficient processing of your daily experiences.

Dream messages are reflections of energy streams from the five segments of the self. With the proper dream knowledge, you can learn to understand the messages from your self-segments. Each message has meaning, just as each experience we have constructs the moments that become our lifetime.

> *The Soul Self*—Soul is the key component of the self. It is imperishable, composed of pure Spirit. It has a design of its own intent and a purpose behind its choice to extend itself into the world of embodiments for experience. When all the selves are integrated, a state of soul infusion exists within us.

> *The Higher Self*—The higher self is the repository of earthly experience culled from the myriad sensory inputs of man as a being. In order to fulfill the soul's purpose for this life we, as the conscious mind, attempt to connect to the wisdom of the higher self and draw on this knowledge to assist us in our day-to-day life.

> *The Emotional Self*—Our emotional self attempts to give us guidance in the form of reactive clues in our daily experiences at work or at

home, with loved ones or co-workers. By learning to understand and work in harmony with the emotional self, we can keep the basic self from working overtime in its attempts to reach our conscious self.

The Basic/Subconscious Self—The basic/subconscious self is the survival self that watches out for our immediate interests; it is also that part of the self that urges us to view issues that we, consciously or unconsciously, have chosen to repress. The shadow self forms part of our basic/subconscious self. It is the part of ourselves that was light and became the darkness in order to serve in our own unfoldment.

The Conscious/Intellectual Self—The conscious self is the state that we can most easily identify with. It is the waking personality that the world knows us by. It is also how the soul's pattern for this life has worked itself down into the matter worlds. The soul self spins the personality into the earth worlds. Our personality is a major part of the waking self (the conscious self).

The soul self and the other self-segments never sleep. They are always communicating to our conscious self through energy streams—especially while we dream. These energy streams are associated with the seven main chakra centers of the etheric body (the chakra system is explained on day 21).

The messages from our self-segments can come as strong and powerful emotive impulses or as subtle vibrational shifts of awareness. As we begin to pay attention to our dreams, we relieve the pressure of backed-up messages and strengthen our conscious ties to the different parts of ourselves. When we make the conscious choice to examine the dream messages from the different parts of ourselves, we take an important step in learning who we are and why we came to earth in this incarnation.

Attuning Your Consciousness to the Guiding Angel

Raphael, archangel of healing, wholeness, and acceptance, will be your guide tonight during your journey into the dream worlds. Before performing tonight's dream exercise, use the following invocation and contemplation to attune yourself to his holy presence.

Invocation to Archangel Raphael

> *Raphael, holy angel of God,*
>   *I desire to know your healing presence. I have made a place*
> *in my heart for your visitation. Come to me in my dreams*
> *tonight and share with me your wisdom and love as I move to*

express my innermost thoughts and feelings. I desire to know
God and to love myself again. Raphael, help me to express and
then heal my pain. I await you in hopeful anticipation of your
radiant presence. Amen.

Allow yourself to feel Raphael's presence enter your heart. Next, to further
attune your consciousness to the guiding presence for tonight, read and contemplate the following words.

> I say unto you, Open your eyes, O man, and fear not the
> truth of thyself. Open your heart, O man, and feel the truth of
> yourself.
>
> —ARCHANGEL RAPHAEL

Allow these words to wash over you. Rest with them for a few minutes and
feel your whole being come into alignment with their truth. Do this for a
few minutes. You have now opened a conduit to the wisdom radiating from
the author of tonight's contemplation—Archangel Raphael. Open your
eyes and continue tonight's session by performing the following dream
exercise.

Tonight's Exercise: Steps toward Inner Healing

It is helpful to review our feelings and thoughts just before going to bed.
Focusing on our thoughts and feelings helps us to get in touch with each part
of our self before entering the dream state. This produces dreams that focus
on integration and wholeness. Spiritual and personal growth always involve
the expression of our thoughts and feelings. In fact, it is imperative we do not
bottle up our reactions to our life experiences.

Try the following exercise before going to bed. It consists of three questions, each designed to help stimulate awareness of your other self-segments.
This will facilitate stronger ties to those segments during your dreams tonight,
resulting in more powerful and clear dream messages.

1. *What are you feeling right now?*
   To begin, simply close your eyes and think about what you feel at this
   moment. Are you relaxed? Is there tension somewhere in your body—
   possibly in your shoulders or neck area? Are you feeling content and
   satisfied, or did something happen today that frustrated you? Identify
   and label your feelings. Then mentally review the major events of your
   day. As you do this, recall the feelings you experienced during these

events. Take a few minutes for this process. Then open your eyes and proceed to the next question.

2. *What are you thinking right now?*
   The nature of our thoughts will often reveal the feeling currents that lie beneath them. When we do not know or cannot acknowledge what we are feeling, it can be helpful to take inventory of our thoughts. Write down some of the thoughts and feelings you had today.

3. *How have your dreams connected you to deeper feelings?*
   Dreams often give us clues to our deeper feelings about important issues in our lives. To uncover these deeper feelings, review your recent dreams. Choose one and write it down. Then identify the feelings that dream invoked in you (e.g., happiness, anxiety, wish-fulfillment). After you have written down your feelings ask yourself what the main "feeling message" of the dream may be.

The focus that this technique creates, especially directly before sleep, should stimulate your self-segments to communicate with you in a more direct manner. As in any relationship, you need to extend your energy by inviting others into your world. Even though the self-segments are parts of you, inviting them into your conscious world is an important step in becoming a fully integrated human being.

———————

Upon awakening in the morning, remember to lie still and keep your eyes closed. Focus your attention on accessing your dream memories. Take some time to allow your dream memories to impress themselves upon your waking mind. After a few minutes, record your dreams in your journal.

When you have finished, begin to unseal the messages hidden within your dreams. Call upon Archangel Raphael to bring you insight as you interpret your dreams by saying the following prayer of invocation.

> *Dear Archangel Raphael,*
> *Send your healing light to illuminate my consciousness that I might better understand the healing messages within my dreams.*
> *Amen.*

Next, perform all seven steps of the interpretation process. The seven steps (from chapter 3) are repeated for you below:

1. Make an inventory or list of each of the characters that appear in your dream, both human and nonhuman.

2. Examine your feelings about the dream characters.

3. Examine your role in the dream and your relationships to the dream characters.

4. Review the actions taking place in the dream.

5. Find out what aspect of yourself the dream characters represent by engaging them in imaginary conversation.

6. Analyze the dream setting (location/time of day/environment).

7. Consider your current life situation.

You will know that you have arrived at the correct dream interpretation when you feel something "click" within you. Don't be discouraged if this doesn't happen right away. The message of your dream may become unsealed over the course of the day or it may take even more time to emerge as you work through your spiritual growth issues.

Meeting Archangel Raphael

Tonight's information will help you to visualize the Archangel Raphael, whose name means "Medicine of God." Raphael's energy helps you to move from repression into a full and complete expression of your feelings, which will promote inner healing as the energy of your heart and the truth of your being are brought into balance.

Archangel Raphael is especially fond of travelers and is usually pictured wearing sandals and holding a walking staff in his left hand. As noted in the book of Tobit, Archangel Raphael escorted a young man named Tobias on a journey. While on the journey, Tobias caught a fish. Raphael instructed Tobias on the medicinal properties of the fish. Tobias later used the liver of the fish to cure his ailing father's eyesight. It was only at the end of the journey that Raphael revealed that he was an archangel of God.

In this story the father represented Tobias's connection to the past. The liver, an organ of cleansing, purified the eyesight of the father by cleansing the impurities and healing the emotional wounds of the past. The emotions are specifically indicated here because the liver came from a fish, a creature of the water. Water commonly symbolizes the emotional nature of man. Thus we see that understanding and accepting our emotions (and learning how to constructively process them) is an important ability to foster within us. Learning to recognize and process our emotions helps us to keep our heart open to the heart of life itself and to all the experiences life offers

Archangel Raphael shows us how to take the step from repression to expression so that we need not spin around in repetitive, conditioned cycles. As we uncover our deepest feelings, we stop trying to be something we're not and we start showing the world and each other who and what we are. Raphael's attributes are healing, wholeness, and acceptance. His process is expressing, and his power is feeling.

Raphael's Dream Message

The following text is from a dream channeling of Archangel Raphael on the topic of dreams.

The healing power of God flows through the energy of the dream worlds. It creates and enlivens your dreams with hidden encoded messages of wholeness and inclusiveness. The message of healing I bring is from the Lord of all Creation—He who has created all matter and provided a place for all men and women to experience the pain and joy of life and to gain the wisdom therein.

The greatest gift our Creator has given us is the power of free will. Without this ability we are unable to be ourselves—our lives would not be what they could be. Believe that there is hope, for the Lord always hears thy pleas. Free expression means freedom in all ways. I ask you to choose integration, rather than repression; and love, rather than fear. Your choice does matter. Look to me and I will send healing energies from the Creator God to you. In the love and light of God.

—RAPHAEL

Attuning Your Consciousness to the Guiding Angel

Raphael, archangel of healing, wholeness, and acceptance, will be your guide tonight during your journey into the dream worlds. Before performing tonight's dream exercise, use the following invocation and contemplation to attune yourself to his holy presence.

Invocation to Archangel Raphael

Raphael, holy angel of God,
   I desire to know your healing presence. I have made a place in my heart for your visitation. Come to me in my dreams tonight and share with me your wisdom and love as I move to express my innermost thoughts and feelings. I desire to know God and to love myself again. Raphael, help me to express and then heal my pain. I await you in hopeful anticipation of your radiant presence. Amen.

Allow yourself to feel Raphael's presence enter your heart. Next, to further attune your consciousness to the guiding presence for tonight, read and contemplate the following words.

Come, and I will show thee the way to thy heart.

—ARCHANGEL RAPHAEL

Allow these words to wash over you. Rest with them for a few minutes and feel your whole being come into alignment with their truth. Do this for a few minutes. You have now opened a conduit to the wisdom radiating from the author of tonight's contemplation—Archangel Raphael. Open your eyes and continue tonight's session by performing the following dream exercise.

Tonight's Exercise: Meeting Archangel Raphael

Archangel Raphael wishes to meet with you in your dream worlds tonight. Many people do not recognize Raphael's power upon meeting him, for his healing energy is like a gentle stream, constantly moving with the life-giving essence of God. The following dream of Linda's will show you what it is like to meet with Raphael in the dream worlds.

Raphael and the Healing Angels

I was in my bed. There was no ceiling above me. Instead I found myself looking at a beautiful blue sky, filled with puffy white clouds. It was daytime, and the sky was a brilliant blue. Suddenly, I noticed a host of angels in the sky, surrounded by the puffy white clouds. I knew that the host of angels were Raphael's healing angels, and I knew it was him in the center of these angels. He was beautifully vibrant, glowing with healing light. Raphael and his angels continued flowing toward me (on a cloud) until they were just a few feet above me. Raphael then said: "I am the Archangel Raphael. You are to work with me."

To help set the tone for your dream meeting with Raphael tonight, relax and repeat the following affirmation several times directly before retiring.

I invite Raphael into my dream worlds tonight. I will remember my dreams of him and his healing angels.

As you repeat this affirmation, feel the presence of Archangel Raphael growing stronger and closer. Continue to repeat the affirmation and gently relax into a deep and restful sleep, knowing that soon you will meet the personage or some aspect of the glorious archangel of God, Raphael, in your dreams.

Upon awakening in the morning, remember to lie still and keep your eyes closed. Focus your attention on accessing your dream memories. Take some time to allow your dream memories to impress themselves upon your waking mind. After a few minutes, record your dreams in your journal.

When you have finished, begin to unseal the messages hidden within your dreams. Call upon Archangel Raphael to bring you insight as you interpret your dreams by saying the following prayer of invocation.

> *Dear Archangel Raphael,*
>   *Send your healing light to illuminate my consciousness that I might better understand the healing messages within my dreams. Amen.*

Next, perform all seven steps of the interpretation process. The seven steps (from chapter 3) are repeated for you below:

1. Make an inventory or list of each of the characters that appear in your dream, both human and nonhuman.
2. Examine your feelings about the dream characters.
3. Examine your role in the dream and your relationships to the dream characters.
4. Review the actions taking place in the dream.
5. Find out what aspect of yourself the dream characters represent by engaging them in imaginary conversation.
6. Analyze the dream setting (location/time of day/environment).
7. Consider your current life situation.

You will know that you have arrived at the correct dream interpretation when you feel something "click" within you. Don't be discouraged if this doesn't happen right away. The message of your dream may become unsealed over the course of the day or it may take even more time to emerge as you work through your spiritual growth issues.

Resolving Recurring Dreams

The theme for tonight is *The Recurring Dream*. Recurring dreams are dreams that insistently draw your attention to an important *need* that is not being fulfilled in your life. Tonight's dream session will help you to understand the underlying purpose of your recurring dreams by unsealing their hidden messages.

Recurring dreams are dreams that you have over and over again. The setting is the same, the characters are the same. During a recurring dream you may have a feeling of déjà vu. These dreams can span a lifetime or occur within a window of weeks or months. Their purpose is to insistently draw your attention to an important *need* that is not being fulfilled in your life.

Recurring dreams can seem quite bothersome, especially if the dream comes as a nightmare or some other uncomfortable experience. But rest assured that recurring dreams contain strong and important messages from one or more of your self-segments. You should pay great heed to analyzing them, for they will continue to knock on the door of your consciousness until you open up and receive them in understanding and acceptance. You can then take conscious steps to fulfill the important need that the recurring dream insists on bringing to your awareness.

We often have recurrent dreams during childhood. As adults we can review those dreams to gain insights into ourselves. Armed with the guidance of the angelic realms we are well equipped to properly apply our discernment to our inner worlds.

The following is Peter's account of a recurring dream from his childhood.

> This recurring dream occurred when I was a young child. In each case, the dream was exactly the same. During the dream a part of me was aware that the dream was occurring. Something about the setting felt familiar—sort of a mild déjà-vu experience. Although a part of me knew what to expect next, I felt that I could not change what was about to happen.

SURPRISE ATTACK

The dream started as I walked along a sidewalk in a nice residential neighborhood. It was a beautiful sunny day. As I walked I began to whistle. Then, out of nowhere, an energy of panic rushed into the dream setting. I became aware that our country was under attack from enemy nuclear missiles. The strange part about this was that the missiles heading for us were somehow caused by me and my whistling. The dream ended with me desperately trying to figure a way out of the impending destruction.

Looking back on this dream I view it as a way that my young mind dealt with the threat of nuclear war—an event that I, as a child, could have no control over. The sunny weather and bright daylight setting of the dream signified that I was consciously aware of the dream issue. My whistling represented an innocent action of joy and happiness. And finally, my fear and guilt over triggering this horrible event most likely was a way to subconsciously feel in control of the situation. In other words, even though I could not figure out how to stop the incoming missiles, I and not an outside unknown force had caused the event. This somehow returned control of my world to me.

I believe that this recurring dream served as a pressure relief valve for my childhood fears of abandonment and nuclear war. The *need* being brought to my attention was the need for security and control over my environment.

You may or may not recall having a recurring dream such as this one. If you haven't, it is still quite possible that a symbol or character has appeared several times in your dreams. You can benefit from identifying the need within you that this symbol or character represents.

When your dream maker sends you recurring dreams, and you still do not take the time to understand the need that is going unfilled, then your dream maker has several options. It can keep sending you the same dream, hoping you'll finally understand its message and take action to fulfill this need. If you still choose to ignore it, and the need is critical to your emotional or physical health, your dream maker can eventually send you a nightmare. This nightmare can turn into a recurring nightmare if you continue to refuse to examine it. Another option your dream maker may resort to is to incorporate a few of the most important recurring elements into a whole new drama that will hopefully draw your attention to the important need.

Tonight's technique will help you to resolve the underlying pressures that may contribute to recurring dreams, or recurring dream symbols. This will relieve your dream maker of the need to continue sending the same messages to your conscious self.

Attuning Your Consciousness to the Guiding Angel

Raphael, archangel of healing, wholeness, and acceptance, will be your guide tonight during your journey into the dream worlds. Before performing tonight's dream exercise, use the following invocation and contemplation to attune yourself to his holy presence.

Invocation to Archangel Raphael

Raphael, holy angel of God,
I desire to know your healing presence. I have made a place
in my heart for your visitation. Come to me in my dreams
tonight and share with me your wisdom and love as I move to
express my innermost thoughts and feelings. I desire to know
God and to love myself again. Raphael, help me to express and
then heal my pain. I await you in hopeful anticipation of your
radiant presence. Amen.

Allow yourself to feel Raphael's presence enter your heart. Next, to further attune your consciousness to the guiding presence for tonight, read and contemplate the following words.

> Expressing your feeling is important for healing.
>
> —ARCHANGEL RAPHAEL

Allow these words to wash over you. Rest with them for a few minutes and feel your whole being come into alignment with their truth. Do this for a few minutes. You have now opened a conduit to the wisdom radiating from the author of tonight's contemplation—Archangel Raphael. Open your eyes and continue tonight's session by performing the following dream exercise.

Tonight's Exercise: Resolving Recurring Dreams

As human beings we have important needs that must be fulfilled in order for us to become a whole, loving, and integrated person. Examples of these needs include the need for connection and intimacy; the need for security; and the need to learn, grow, and expand.

Our unmet needs tend to create blocks within us that prevent us from feeling love for others (and ourselves). They also prevent us from freely extending our love and our gifts to others. Until we become aware of our needs and take steps to fulfill them, it is unlikely that we can reach our full potential.

Raphael, the archangel of healing, wholeness, and acceptance, will help you examine and understand the recurring elements within your dreams tonight. The following exercise will help you to identify and take steps to fulfill an important need that is not being met in your life.

1. Upon retiring, think about a recurring dream or a recurring dream symbol you have had. You can choose a recent dream or pick one from your childhood. If you are having trouble finding a recurring symbol, try looking through some of your old dream journals.

2. After you have chosen the dream or dream symbol that you wish to focus on, repeat the following affirmation several times:

   The meaning of my recurring dream symbols will become clear to me tonight. I will work with Archangel Raphael to understand the important need that is going unfulfilled in my life.

As you repeat this affirmation, feel the presence of Archangel Raphael growing stronger and closer. Continue to repeat the affirmation as you gently relax into a deep and restful sleep, knowing that soon you will have a dream that unveils the cause or meaning of a recurring dream or dream symbol.

———————

Upon awakening in the morning, remember to lie still and keep your eyes closed. Focus your attention on accessing your dream memories. Take some time to allow your dream memories to impress themselves upon your waking mind. After a few minutes, record your dreams in your journal.

When you have finished, begin to unseal the messages hidden within your dreams. Call upon Archangel Raphael to bring you insight as you interpret your dreams by saying the following prayer of invocation.

   Dear Archangel Raphael,
   Send your healing light to illuminate my consciousness that I might better understand the healing messages within my dreams. Amen.

Next, perform all seven steps of the interpretation process. The seven steps (from chapter 3) are repeated for you below:

1. Make an inventory or list of each of the characters that appear in your dream, both human and nonhuman.

2. Examine your feelings about the dream characters.

3. Examine your role in the dream and your relationships to the dream characters.

4. Review the actions taking place in the dream.

5. Find out what aspect of yourself the dream characters represent by engaging them in imaginary conversation.

6. Analyze the dream setting (location/time of day/environment).

7. Consider your current life situation.

You will know that you have arrived at the correct dream interpretation when you feel something "click" within you. Don't be discouraged if this doesn't happen right away. The message of your dream may become unsealed over the course of the day or it may take even more time to emerge as you work through your spiritual growth issues.

DAY 11

Dream of Healing

Tonight you will continue to work with Archangel Raphael as he helps you learn how to incubate a dream of healing. We usually think of healing as the healing of our physical body, but most healing occurs first in the inner realms. Raphael will help you to heal your inner self by uncovering wounds from your past and applying the healing salve of God's grace on them. He will show you how to use the dream worlds to facilitate inner healing.

Dreams bring healing to us in many different ways. They make us aware of hidden traumas and feelings of guilt that our conscious mind needs to examine, understand, forgive, and release. Dreams point out self-destructive patterns, just as they provide healing solutions for these tendencies. In each case, healing comes about through an increased level of awareness within us that unwinds patterns that bind us to dis-ease.

We need to pay attention to our dreams; they have the power to lead us to a state of healing and wholeness. They are an important source of self-knowledge, which is vital in the healing process. The self-awareness that our dreams bring to us is free for the asking. It is available to us every time we sleep.

As you move toward integration, a large part of your dream work will involve healing the aspect of yourself that feels separate and cut off from God the Creator. Heeding the healing messages within your dreams will help you to reclaim your heritage as a child of God—to realize that you are soul, created from the very substance of God's light.

Much of your inner pain will be dissolved in the holy water of self-forgiveness as your healing dreams reveal the fears and misunderstandings that have kept you from accepting your higher nature. As you move past your feelings of unworthiness, you can then step into your power—the power of your soul, whose dream messages can create as well as heal.

The following example of a self-healing dream uses past-life images to promote healing. Our dreams can access *any* of our life experiences—past, present, or even future—as they lead us on our journey to wholeness.

In this dream Linda's healing is facilitated by herself and two of her good friends who have never met in the waking world reality. One of these friends, Mary, had died before the time of the dream.

THE HEALING SESSION

I dreamed that I was in the kitchen of a very large house. My friends Sue and Mary were there too. I was so happy to see Mary again. (She had passed to the spirit realms more than a decade earlier.) I hugged her and seemed to melt right into her wonderful energy. It felt so healing to see her and be near her again; this was only the second time I'd dreamed of her since her death.

I drank in the vision of Mary, so tall, so beautiful. She was more focused than I had ever seen her before. She had a purpose for being in my dream—I knew it was to assist in my healing process.

I was so happy that my friends Sue and Mary could finally meet. It did not matter that this meeting took place in a dream or that Mary was dead. They had both come for the same purpose: to facilitate my healing process.

The healing session began as Mary and Sue directed my attention to scenes being displayed in an adjoining room. I could see actual living images of myself on a screen in that room. The first to appear on the screen were images of myself as a child; these seemed to be living, breathing images. In the scene I played with toys. The images were not flat but were three-dimensional, whole, and incredibly real. I found it very healing to see myself as a child, an innocent two-year-old.

Then my friends directed me to look at another scene. I again saw a two-year-old child who looked somewhat like me, but the energy was different around this child. The energy seemed to be more focused and directed than mine. I didn't know why until my friends showed me scenes of a young man (age twenty-five to thirty) and a slightly older man (around forty). They were clearly the same man. He was blond like the child, and he had a large mustache, kind eyes, and a nice smile.

Mary wanted me to understand something. Finally something clicked within me, and I realized that I was (or had been) this young male child and I had grown up to become the blond man. They were images of me in my most recent past life.

> *I knew that my goal in this healing session was to simply look upon these images and absorb the energy and life force that emanated from my former self.*
>
> *As I gazed at these living images, I knew I had much to learn from them. I could feel the grace of God as I absorbed the healing and the knowledge of this, my former life.*

The above example is one way in which our dreams work to help heal our psyches. This particular dream used past life imagery to spur healing and wholeness within Linda. Linda was aware and lucid within the dream. She knew that her friends were there with her to help facilitate this healing session. Connecting with the energy and feelings from past life experiences can help us understand our patterns and motivations in this present life.

You can make the choice now to heed the messages contained within your dreams, for dreams exist as a service to you. They bring the lost parts of yourself into wholeness and help you to contact the realms of God where your soul self resides.

Attuning Your Consciousness to the Guiding Angel

Raphael, archangel of healing, wholeness, and acceptance, will be your guide tonight during your journey into the dream worlds. Before performing tonight's dream exercise, use the following invocation and contemplation to attune yourself to his holy presence.

Invocation to Archangel Raphael

> *Raphael, holy angel of God,*
> *I desire to know your healing presence. I have made a place in my heart for your visitation. Come to me in my dreams tonight and share with me your wisdom and love as I move to express my innermost thoughts and feelings. I desire to know God and to love myself again. Raphael, help me to express and then heal my pain. I await you in hopeful anticipation of your radiant presence. Amen.*

Allow yourself to feel Raphael's presence enter your heart. Next, to further attune your consciousness to the guiding presence for tonight, read and contemplate the following words.

> The healing that you seek is not the healing of the body
> alone, but the return to the heart of God.
>
> —ARCHANGEL RAPHAEL

Allow these words to wash over you. Rest with them for a few minutes and feel your whole being come into alignment with their truth. Do this for a few minutes. You have now opened a conduit to the wisdom radiating from the author of tonight's contemplation—Archangel Raphael. Open your eyes and continue tonight's session by performing the following dream exercise.

Tonight's Exercise: Dream of Healing

Healing reflects a state of balance and comes on many levels—physical, emotional, intellectual, and spiritual. Raphael's healing energy will soothe and bring healing to some area of your life during your dreams tonight. Many have petitioned his help and so can you.

Upon retiring relax and close your eyes. Next, choose one main area of your life that you feel needs healing and wholeness—either a physical or an emotional need. After you have chosen your area for healing recite the following prayer several times.

> *Dear Archangel Raphael—angel of healing, wholeness, and acceptance,*
> *Please come to me in my dreams tonight. I need your help to heal _____ (state your need). I await your loving presence. This I ask of you through the universal Christ energy. Amen.*

As you repeat the prayer feel the presence of Archangel Raphael growing stronger and closer. Continue to repeat the prayer and gently relax into a deep and restful sleep, knowing that soon you will have a dream of healing that will resolve a known or unknown tension within you.

Upon awakening in the morning, remember to lie still and keep your eyes closed. Focus your attention on accessing your dream memories. Take some time to allow your dream memories to impress themselves upon your waking mind. After a few minutes, record your dreams in your journal.

When you have finished, begin to unseal the messages hidden within your dreams. Call upon Archangel Raphael to bring you insight as you interpret your dreams by saying the following prayer of invocation.

> *Dear Archangel Raphael,*
> *Send your healing light to illuminate my consciousness that I*

might better understand the healing messages within my dreams. Amen.

Next, perform all seven steps of the interpretation process. The seven steps (from chapter 3) are repeated for you below:

1. Make an inventory or list of each of the characters that appear in your dream, both human and nonhuman.
2. Examine your feelings about the dream characters.
3. Examine your role in the dream and your relationships to the dream characters.
4. Review the actions taking place in the dream.
5. Find out what aspect of yourself the dream characters represent by engaging them in imaginary conversation.
6. Analyze the dream setting (location/time of day/environment).
7. Consider your current life situation.

You will know that you have arrived at the correct dream interpretation when you feel something "click" within you. Don't be discouraged if this doesn't happen right away. The message of your dream may become unsealed over the course of the day or it may take even more time to emerge as you work through your spiritual growth issues.

Problem Solving in Relationships

Relationships are perhaps the most important facet of our life on Earth. It has been said that no man is an island. This being true, it behooves us to focus on solving our relationship problems. As you will learn tonight, the dream worlds offer you the perfect environment for working out your relationship problems. As a part of tonight's dream session, we will also discuss the related topic of wish-fulfillment dreams.

Dreams provide an environment that is especially suited for solving relationship problems. Whether you are aware of it or not, you have probably already had many dreams in which your inner self has attempted to resolve relationship problems. Such dreams can refer to your relationship with yourself, such as when you need to come to terms with a situation or decision you must make. Or they can refer to your relationships with others. Relationship dreams should therefore be considered on at least two levels.

On the first level, consider the dream characters as extensions of yourself. The characters will tell you what you need to know about yourself. As you interpret your dream on this level, ask yourself the following questions: How do the dream characters appear (happy, angry, depressed)? Who do they remind me of? How am I like these characters? Which of these characters' qualities do I like and which do I dislike? In this way you gain deeper insights into aspects of your personality that you might wish to change.

On the second level, consider the dream characters as extensions of your waking-world relationship partners. Their purpose is to help you process emotional residue in the dream state. This is especially common during traumatic times, such as divorce or a health crisis. The predominant factor in these dreams is that you interact with the individual(s) almost as if you were in the normal waking state. In other words, the issues that come up reflect waking-world relationship problems. Considering dreams on this level can generate genuine realizations and emotional energy shifts within you.

In relationship dreams we give our repressed fears free rein to express themselves. We find ourselves speaking and acting in ways that we are afraid to in our normal waking life. In this way we can play out scenarios with our relationship partners (current or former) that we would never experience in our real life. We can learn and grow from this role-playing opportunity. After awakening from this type of dream, we become aware of steps that we can take to create positive changes in our lives.

Wish upon a Dream—Wish-Fulfillment Dreams

A wish-fulfillment dream highlights some aspect of life that you long to change or to experience. These dreams are characteristically positive and uplifting. During a wish-fulfillment dream something that you deeply desire to experience can be made real—if only in your dreams.

Within the environment of such dreams, events occur that you know could not happen—if they did happen, they would be considered miraculous. For example, if one is disabled and then is suddenly able to walk; or blind and then able to see.

A wish-fulfillment dream can also represent getting something you want, such as a new house. Through such dreams, you can have an experience that you greatly desire. For example, if you love to fly but do not have the time or money for the real experience, your dream maker can provide it for you. Or, if you are homesick for a particular place, you will find it recreated for you though the miracle of a wish-fulfillment dream.

The flip side to wish-fulfillment dreams are dreams of relief. Upon awakening from such a dream, one is usually very relieved to find that the dream was *not* reality. For example, you may dream of the death of a loved one, and the dream's energy has such strength that it elicits great waves of sadness and desperation. Usually you are not aware that you are dreaming. It is only when you awaken that you find that what you thought was real was thankfully only a dream.

Dreams of relief are actually opportunities to review our life and our priorities. They offer us the chance to repair our relationships with others before it is too late. Like Ebenezer Scrooge's dream of Christmas future in Dickens's *A Christmas Carol*, dreams of relief offer us a chance to change. They elicit within us a deep sense of appreciation and gratitude for the blessings that are already present in our life.

Attuning Your Consciousness to the Guiding Angel

Raphael, archangel of healing, wholeness, and acceptance, will be your guide tonight during your journey into the dream worlds. Before performing tonight's dream exercise, use the following invocation and contemplation to attune yourself to his holy presence.

Invocation to Archangel Raphael

> *Raphael, holy angel of God,*
> *I desire to know your healing presence. I have made a place*
> *in my heart for your visitation. Come to me in my dreams*
> *tonight and share with me your wisdom and love as I move to*
> *express my innermost thoughts and feelings. I desire to heal my*
> *relationships and bring harmony to my life. Raphael, help me to*
> *forgive myself and others. I await you in hopeful anticipation of*
> *your radiant presence. Amen.*

Allow yourself to feel Raphael's presence enter your heart. Next, to further attune your consciousness to the guiding presence for tonight, read and contemplate the following words.

> May the love within you flower and heal the wounds of life
> and enliven you with divine energy and peace.
>
> —ARCHANGEL RAPHAEL

Allow these words to wash over you. Rest with them for a few minutes and feel your whole being come into alignment with their truth. Do this for a few minutes. You have now opened a conduit to the wisdom radiating from the author of tonight's contemplation—Archangel Raphael. Open your eyes and continue tonight's session by performing the following dream exercise.

Tonight's Exercise: Problem Solving in Relationships

Tonight you will receive an answer to a problem you are having in one of your relationships. Whether your problem is small or large, your self-segments and the angels will present you with keys and clues to help you learn and grow.

Upon retiring tonight, relax and close your eyes. Next, choose the relationship that needs your attention. Consider the situation for a few moments then repeat the following affirmation several times.

> **Tonight in my dreams I will receive an answer regarding**
> _____ **(state your problem).**
> **The messages from my self-segments and the angels will be clear,**
> **helpful, and healing to all concerned.**

As you repeat this affirmation, feel the presence of Archangel Raphael growing stronger and closer. Continue to repeat the affirmation and gently relax into a deep and restful sleep knowing that soon you will have a dream that will bring you an answer to help you resolve your relationship problem.

Upon awakening in the morning, remember to lie still and keep your eyes closed. Focus your attention on accessing your dream memories. Take some time to allow your dream memories to impress themselves upon your waking mind. After a few minutes, record your dreams in your journal.

When you have finished, begin to unseal the messages hidden within your dreams. Call upon Archangel Raphael to bring you insight as you interpret your dreams by saying the following prayer of invocation.

> *Dear Archangel Raphael,*
> *Send your healing light to illuminate my consciousness that I might better understand the healing messages within my dreams. Amen.*

Next, perform all seven steps of the interpretation process. The seven steps (from chapter 3) are repeated for you below:

1. Make an inventory or list of each of the characters that appear in your dream, both human and nonhuman.
2. Examine your feelings about the dream characters.
3. Examine your role in the dream and your relationships to the dream characters.
4. Review the actions taking place in the dream.
5. Find out what aspect of yourself the dream characters represent by engaging them in imaginary conversation.
6. Analyze the dream setting (location/time of day/environment).
7. Consider your current life situation.

You will know that you have arrived at the correct dream interpretation when you feel something "click" within you. Don't be discouraged if this doesn't happen right away. The message of your dream may become unsealed over the course of the day or it may take even more time to emerge as you work through your spiritual growth issues.

Meeting Archangel Gabriel

Now that the soothing energies of Archangel Raphael have helped you to open and begin to heal your heart, the time has come to work with Archangel Gabriel's dynamic energy of accomplishment. Tonight you will meet this glorious angel in your dream worlds. As you work with Gabriel over the next few days, you will discover a renewed strength of purpose that will help you to fulfill your mission for this lifetime.

St. Gabriel, the archangel best known for his appearance to the Virgin Mary, is often depicted carrying a scepter in his right hand. The scepter is symbolic of the transfer of power from the Creator to the one whom this holy angel visits. In what is called the annunciation, Gabriel communicated a message from the Creator to Mary. He informed Mary that God had chosen her as the pure vessel to carry the Christ child. Mary was offered this honor and was given the choice to accept or decline.

Gabriel is the symbolic messenger for each of us as we are presented with the task of choosing our particular mission for this lifetime. Like Mary, we can either accept or decline. Just as the final runner in a relay race is handed the baton, we are handed the scepter of Gabriel. It is then up to us to proceed toward our end goal. This symbolic transfer of power focuses with the full force of reality on the fact that it is you who must choose your specific life's mission and you who must take conscious steps toward the completion of that mission.

Gabriel helps us to remove the inner blocks that keep us from action. Without action we cannot affect the forms and substances around us. In order to create change in our lives, we must engage life. When faced with our internal blocks, we can either waver back in fear or move forward with courage.

We can most strongly feel Gabriel's influence after we have worked with Archangel Michael to unravel our individual conditioning and with Archangel Raphael to express our true feelings in constructive and ultimately healing ways. Gabriel's attributes are strength, commitment, and persistence. His process is accomplishment, and his power is acting.

Gabriel's Dream Message

The following text comes from a channeling of Archangel Gabriel on the topic of dreams.

> Your dream worlds are constructed from the interaction of energy from within you and from the energy of others around you. Your life choices are like pebbles thrown upon the pond. Each move you make affects the energy streams of the world. We are all in a sea of God's energy. We are all interconnected to each other. Our actions are therefore important to each other. What one person does affects all humanity. And what one person does *not* do affects all of humanity as well.
>
> If you wish to build a purposeful life call upon me. I will come to you in your dreams and encourage you in your efforts to understand the mysterious language of your inner worlds. Communicating with your self-segments is a sacred undertaking. Approach it with the sincerity and reverence you would any love interest—for how can you fully love another until you love and accept yourself? Unconditional love is the root of happiness. In the light and love of the Creator.
>
> —GABRIEL

Attuning Your Consciousness to the Guiding Angel

Gabriel, messenger of God, will be your guide tonight during your journey into the dream worlds. Before performing tonight's dream exercise, use the following invocation and contemplation to attune yourself to his holy presence.

Invocation to Archangel Gabriel

> *Gabriel, holy angel of God,*
>   *I ask you to come to me in my dreams tonight. Imbue me with the power of your strength as I commit to you my desire to create change in my life and to manifest my life's mission. In my dreams I will make a place for our meeting. With courage I will meet you, and with courage I will take steps to bring into manifestation my mission in an effort to complete my soul's purpose and pattern for this lifetime. Amen.*

Allow yourself to feel Gabriel's presence enter your heart. Next, to further attune your consciousness to the guiding presence for tonight, read and contemplate the following words.

> "Commitment begins with the joining of hands, the clasping of arms, and the choice to walk the fields together as we plow and plant the seeds of creation unto the earth.
>
> —Archangel Gabriel

Allow these words to wash over you. Rest with them for a few minutes and feel your whole being come into alignment with their truth. Do this for a few minutes. You have now opened a conduit to the wisdom radiating from the author of tonight's contemplation—Archangel Gabriel. Open your eyes and continue tonight's session by performing the following dream exercise.

Tonight's Exercise: Meeting Archangel Gabriel

Archangel Gabriel wishes to meet with you in your dream worlds tonight. Gabriel has appeared to people as both a male angel and a female angel. When meeting him, one can sense the strength of purpose that emanates from him. To help set the tone for meeting Gabriel, relax and repeat the following affirmation several times directly before retiring.

> **I accept my personal strength and commit to the task of understanding my dream worlds with the help of the holy Archangel Gabriel. I await him in my dream worlds tonight.**

As you repeat this affirmation, feel the presence of Archangel Gabriel growing stronger and closer. Continue to repeat the affirmation and gently relax into a deep and restful sleep, knowing that soon you will meet the personage or some aspect of the glorious archangel of God, Gabriel, in your dreams.

Upon awakening in the morning, remember to lie still and keep your eyes closed. Focus your attention on accessing your dream memories. Take some time to allow your dream memories to impress themselves upon your waking mind. After a few minutes, record your dreams in your journal.

When you have finished, begin to unseal the messages hidden within your dreams. Call upon Archangel Gabriel to bring you insight as you interpret your dreams by saying the following prayer of invocation.

Dear Archangel Gabriel,
*   I ask that your messages be clear and your presence strong as*
I interpret my dreams today. I trust in your guidance and
accept your divine help. I commit myself to the process of per-
sonal growth and the accomplishment of my personal mission.
Amen.

Next, perform all seven steps of the interpretation process. The seven steps (from chapter 3) are repeated for you below:

1. Make an inventory or list of each of the characters that appear in your dream, both human and nonhuman.
2. Examine your feelings about the dream characters.
3. Examine your role in the dream and your relationships to the dream characters.
4. Review the actions taking place in the dream.
5. Find out what aspect of yourself the dream characters represent by engaging them in imaginary conversation.
6. Analyze the dream setting (location/time of day/environment).
7. Consider your current life situation.

You will know that you have arrived at the correct dream interpretation when you feel something "click" within you. Don't be discouraged if this doesn't happen right away. The message of your dream may become unsealed over the course of the day or it may take even more time to emerge as you work through your spiritual growth issues.

Dream of Strength

Now that you have met with Archangel Gabriel in the dream worlds, you are ready to explore his main virtue: strength. With strength you can accomplish your goals—material and spiritual. Tonight's dream topic will explain how you can increase your spiritual strength by applying Gabriel's secondary virtues: persistence and commitment.

Strength is built within you as a by-product of the conscious application of the divine attributes of persistence and commitment. Without these attributes, very few great inventions or deep spiritual and philosophical insights would have been possible.

As an illustration of how persistence and commitment interact, imagine that you have decided to begin a weight-lifting program to increase your physical strength. If your exercise routine consisted of lifting a thirty-pound dumbbell only one time, what results could you expect to see reflected in your body over time? Very little.

Even though you may run through your exercise period every day of the year, your results will be minimal. While you have shown commitment (exercising every day of the year), you have not persisted in lifting the dumbbell enough times during each exercise period to gain real results.

On the flip side imagine that you lift that thirty-pound dumbbell 250 times during each exercise period. But in this example, instead of exercising every day, you only exercise once a month. What kind of results can you expect? Most likely you would still find minimal change in your strength because your level of commitment has been low.

If you have trouble relating to this weight-lifting scenario, consider the same concepts as they apply to dieting. For example, if you followed your weight-loss diet only one hour a day over the course of a year (and ate whatever you wanted the rest of the time) what results could you expect? Conversely, if you dieted twenty-four hours a day, but only one day a month, what results could you expect at the end of the year?

Building strength takes both persistence (concentrated focused energy) and commitment (focusing that energy consistently over time). These two attributes are vital in building our spiritual, mental, and emotional strength. When you meditate, pray, and actively focus on the angels consistently, for a long enough time period each day, you will quite naturally build the inner strength you need to carry you through to the completion of your life's mission.

If your goal (mission) in the weight-lifting example were to increase your physical strength so that you could swim the English channel, your odds of success would have been far greater if you had chosen to exercise for thirty minutes every day of the year.

Just as the principles of persistence and commitment apply to the accomplishment of physical goals through building strength, they also apply to the preparation necessary to fulfill your life's mission. Archangel Gabriel inspires you to continue your inner strength building so that you can accomplish that mission. Look to him in your meditations, dreams, and prayers when you feel weak and in need of the power of God. Bit by bit and day by day, you will grow in strength. This will, in turn, have a multiplying effect on achieving your life goals. With your newly developed strength you will find it easier to work on all aspects of your mission.

Attuning Your Consciousness to the Guiding Angel

Gabriel, messenger of God, will be your guide tonight during your journey into the dream worlds. Before performing tonight's dream exercise, use the following invocation and contemplation to attune yourself to his holy presence.

Invocation to Archangel Gabriel

> *Gabriel, holy angel of God,*
> *I ask you to come to me in my dreams tonight. Imbue me*
> *with the power of your strength as I commit to you my desire to*
> *create change in my life and to manifest my life's mission. In*
> *my dreams I will make a place for our meeting. With courage I*
> *will meet you, and with courage I will take steps to bring into*
> *manifestation my mission in an effort to complete my soul's pur-*
> *pose and pattern for this lifetime. Amen.*

Allow yourself to feel Gabriel's presence enter your heart. Next, to further attune your consciousness to the guiding presence for tonight, read and contemplate the following words.

> As the painful scars dissolve in the water of the Holy Spirit, you are now ready to define, begin, carry out, and complete your soul's purpose—your mission for this lifetime.
>
> —Archangel Gabriel

Allow these words to wash over you. Rest with them for a few minutes and feel your whole being come into alignment with their truth. Do this for a few minutes. You have now opened a conduit to the wisdom radiating from the author of tonight's contemplation—Archangel Gabriel. Open your eyes and continue tonight's session by performing the following dream exercise.

Tonight's Exercise: Dream of Strength

Gabriel is archangel of strength, commitment, and persistence. Tonight you will have a dream influenced by Gabriel's energy. It will focus on the virtue of strength in your life. Your dream may also reflect aspects of commitment and persistence.

As you go to sleep tonight think about your life for a few minutes. Think about your successes and your failures. Choose one area of your life that you wish you were stronger in—an area that you would change if you felt you could. Next, repeat the following prayer to Gabriel several times.

> Dear Archangel Gabriel,
>   I desire to grow in strength in order to accomplish my life's mission. Please show me how I can strengthen _____ (state your choice) in my dreams tonight. Amen.

As you repeat the prayer, allow yourself to feel Gabriel's presence. Know that Gabriel will illuminate your dreams with the energy of strength. Gently relax and fall into a deep restful sleep.

———————

Upon awakening in the morning, remember to lie still and keep your eyes closed. Focus your attention on accessing your dream memories. Take some time to allow your dream memories to impress themselves upon your waking mind. After a few minutes, record your dreams in your journal.

When you have finished, begin to unseal the messages hidden within your dreams. Call upon Archangel Gabriel to bring you insight as you interpret your dreams by saying the following prayer of invocation.

Dear Archangel Gabriel,
    I ask that your messages be clear and your presence strong as
I interpret my dreams today. I trust in your guidance and
accept your divine help. I commit myself to the process of personal growth and the accomplishment of my personal mission.
Amen.

Next, perform all seven steps of the interpretation process. The seven steps (from chapter 3) are repeated for you below:

1. Make an inventory or list of each of the characters that appear in your dream, both human and nonhuman.
2. Examine your feelings about the dream characters.
3. Examine your role in the dream and your relationships to the dream characters.
4. Review the actions taking place in the dream.
5. Find out what aspect of yourself the dream characters represent by engaging them in imaginary conversation.
6. Analyze the dream setting (location/time of day/environment).
7. Consider your current life situation.

You will know that you have arrived at the correct dream interpretation when you feel something "click" within you. Don't be discouraged if this doesn't happen right away. The message of your dream may become unsealed over the course of the day or it may take even more time to emerge as you work through your spiritual growth issues.

DAY 15

Dreaming Your Life's Mission

Finding meaning and purpose in our lives is important. We all want to feel that we are fulfilling the purpose for which we have come to Earth. Tonight's dream topic and exercise can help stimulate new insights that will assist you in defining and accomplishing your life's mission.

What is our life's mission? In a nutshell it is the major purpose for our incarnation into this lifetime on Earth. It is our destiny—our reason for being here. Sometimes our mission is found in the occupation we have chosen. Fortunate are those who can earn their way in this world by carrying out their life's mission. Yet more often we must exert extra effort (after hours) to fulfill our true mission.

A mission can be life-long or last for only a specific time frame. For example, a lifetime mission could take the form of practicing the healing arts through ongoing progressive studies, while a specific time frame mission may include writing a book on a particular subject.

Manifesting Our Dreams

All that we see in the world was begotten from a dream. God's dream was the first dream. In His infinite grace He has given each of us the power to dream, and that power is the defining attribute of humanity. All the great cities and modern marvels, the artwork of the masters, and the architecture of the glorious cathedrals in Europe were once only thoughts in the minds of men. Yet even before they were thoughts, they were first dreams.

Fed with enthusiasm from the dream worlds, our thoughts can focus energy into physical matter, thus creating a solid physical reality that manifests in this world. This enables us to accomplish our life's mission.

How can we generate this enthusiasm? Often, you only need to start taking active steps toward your goal. You will then find that your energy level begins to increase, resulting in higher levels of excitement regarding your goal.

A task not yet started can look like an impossibility. We feel the weight of the effort necessary to perform the task and we sense only the "hardness" and perceived difficulties. We must learn instead to sense the positive feelings of joy and accomplishment that will come as we fulfill our chosen tasks.

This repatterning of ourselves energizes us. We become open to the life force as we choose to actively join in the process. For although the "water" may seem too cold and we resist jumping in, it's not that bad once we do. In fact, once we become immersed in the process we usually do enjoy ourselves. For example, while it may be hard to part with money to pay for a European vacation, we know the effort (in the expenditure of our hard earned cash) will be well worth the learning experiences we will gain as a result of journeying to a foreign land.

This repatterning of our attitude is precisely the same technique we need to employ in defining and dreaming our life's mission. We need to move from focusing on the weight of the task ahead to focusing on the state that we will find ourselves in once we have achieved our mission. Like a magnifying glass that focuses the energy of the sun to start a fire, your concentrated focus on your life's mission will light the fire of your consciousness. This flame will burn in your heart and soul so brightly that your life will be full of adventure, love, and excitement. So take heart and know that your goals are obtainable in this lifetime.

Attuning Your Consciousness to the Guiding Angel

Gabriel, messenger of God, will be your guide tonight during your journey into the dream worlds. Before performing tonight's dream exercise, use the following invocation and contemplation to attune yourself to his holy presence.

Invocation to Archangel Gabriel

> Gabriel, holy angel of God,
>   I ask you to come to me in my dreams tonight. Imbue me
> with the power of your strength as I commit to you my desire to
> create change in my life and to manifest my life's mission. In
> my dreams I will make a place for our meeting. With courage I
> will meet you, and with courage I will take steps to bring into
> manifestation my mission in an effort to complete my soul's purpose and pattern for this lifetime. Amen.

Allow yourself to feel Gabriel's presence enter your heart. Next, to further attune your consciousness to the guiding presence for tonight, read and contemplate the following words.

It is commitment to your soul self and to God that will carry you through to the completion of your mission, whatever it may be.

—ARCHANGEL GABRIEL

Allow these words to wash over you. Rest with them for a few minutes and feel your whole being come into alignment with their truth. Do this for a few minutes. You have now opened a conduit to the wisdom radiating from the author of tonight's contemplation—Archangel Gabriel. Open your eyes and continue tonight's session by performing the following dream exercise.

Tonight's Exercise: Dreaming Your Life's Mission

Are you on track with your life's mission? Perhaps you haven't yet figured out what your mission is. Tonight you'll receive guidance in your dreams from your soul self at the direction of Archangel Gabriel. Your soul's messages will help you to uncover your life's mission and how well you are presently fulfilling it.

Begin tonight's exercise by imagining your soul self as a golden ball of pure light. Reach out in your mind's eye and embrace this holy part of yourself. As you imagine this, repeat the following affirmation several times. It will help set the tone for your night's dreams.

I wish to see, know, and feel how well I am accomplishing my mission. I look to my soul self, holder of the blueprint of my life, to show me the answer in my dreams tonight.

As you repeat this affirmation, feel the presence of your soul self growing stronger. Continue to repeat the affirmation and gently relax into a deep and restful sleep knowing that soon you will learn more about your life's mission and how to accomplish it.

Upon awakening in the morning, remember to lie still and keep your eyes closed. Focus your attention on accessing your dream memories. Take some time to allow your dream memories to impress themselves upon your waking mind. After a few minutes, record your dreams in your journal.

When you have finished, begin to unseal the messages hidden within your dreams. Call upon Archangel Gabriel to bring you insight as you interpret your dreams by saying the following prayer of invocation.

Dear Archangel Gabriel,
    I ask that your messages be clear and your presence strong as I interpret my dreams today. I trust in your guidance and accept your divine help. I commit myself to the process of personal growth and the accomplishment of my personal mission. Amen.

Next, perform all seven steps of the interpretation process. The seven steps (from chapter 3) are repeated for you below:

1. Make an inventory or list of each of the characters that appear in your dream, both human and nonhuman.
2. Examine your feelings about the dream characters.
3. Examine your role in the dream and your relationships to the dream characters.
4. Review the actions taking place in the dream.
5. Find out what aspect of yourself the dream characters represent by engaging them in imaginary conversation.
6. Analyze the dream setting (location/time of day/environment).
7. Consider your current life situation.

You will know that you have arrived at the correct dream interpretation when you feel something "click" within you. Don't be discouraged if this doesn't happen right away. The message of your dream may become unsealed over the course of the day or it may take even more time to emerge as you work through your spiritual growth issues.

DAY 16

Acting on the Dream Stage

Each part of your self has a role to play in carrying out your life's mission. As actors on a stage work together to present a story to the audience, your self-segments work together on the dream stage to assist you in performing your chosen mission. We finish tonight's dream session with an exercise that will stimulate your dream maker to create dreams relating to how your choice of a life's mission will affect you and the lives of those around you.

Have you ever just wanted the world to stop so that you could get off for a while? Have you ever wished to know what lies beyond the veil of death? For centuries humanity has searched for the meaning of life and run away from the fear that when the earthly body died consciousness would also dissipate. Even though many have feared death, the unknown (that which lies beyond the view of our physical senses) holds a strange fascination.

This desire to stop the world, to reach the "end" as quickly as possible, is actually a reflection of what is termed *the death wish,* an unconscious drive within us that seeks to end life and discover an ultimate state of rest. It also reflects a desire to explore afterlife possibilities as a spiritual being. Like a reader of a suspense novel who cannot help but look at the final pages to uncover the ending, we, at times, desire to complete the play and look behind the curtain to see the underlying reality of life.

Yet, as in a play, we each have a part to portray, a costume to wear, and lines to read in the scenes of our life. Adventure is afoot, and we are in the center of our creation. One of the reasons we have chosen to come to Earth is to experience—to participate! If you're bored with your scenes, you can change your costume by modifying your patterns. This will help you to move into new realms of experience. You don't have to die to change your life—you simply have to live with all the passion your heart can generate.

Gabriel will help you gain the strength to pull yourself into the moment. This is the space where there is no tomorrow and no yesterday. All that is, has always been, and will always be contained in the mystery of each moment of existence. When you are feeling down and discouraged, call on Gabriel, for he will inject the liquid energy of God into your aura, rejuvenating your will to live.

Remember that while your conscious self is participating in the play of life, your self-segments (each wearing its own costume) are participating as well. Learning to recognize their roles and understanding the motivations for their actions is part of what keeps us excited about life's possibilities. It is also a key to achieving penetrating dream interpretation skills.

When you feel unsure of the direction you should take in your outer life, you can rely on your inner dream worlds to provide you with feedback. This feedback will come from each part of your self and from the angelic realms.

Your dream worlds provide a flexible and safe place to play out your future physical choices without the pain of learning the hard way. Tonight's exercise will show you how to use your dream worlds to gain guidance and clues about which direction to take.

Attuning Your Consciousness to the Guiding Angel

Gabriel, messenger of God, will be your guide tonight during your journey into the dream worlds. Before performing tonight's dream exercise, use the following invocation and contemplation to attune yourself to his holy presence.

Invocation to Archangel Gabriel

> Gabriel, holy angel of God,
>   I ask you to come to me in my dreams tonight. Imbue me
> with the power of your strength as I commit to you my desire to
> create change in my life and to manifest my life's mission. In
> my dreams I will make a place for our meeting. With courage I
> will meet you, and with courage I will take steps to bring into
> manifestation my mission in an effort to complete my soul's pur-
> pose and pattern for this lifetime. Amen.

Allow yourself to feel Gabriel's presence enter your heart. Next, to further attune your consciousness to the guiding presence for tonight, read and contemplate the following words.

> All beings shape and move energy. The musician takes his
> energy and transmutes it through the body of his instrument,
> which in turns moves the energy of the atoms in the atmos-
> phere creating sound.

> —ARCHANGEL GABRIEL

Allow these words to wash over you. Rest with them for a few minutes and feel your whole being come into alignment with their truth. Do this for a few minutes. You have now opened a conduit to the wisdom radiating from the author of tonight's contemplation—Archangel Gabriel. Open your eyes and continue tonight's session by performing the following dream exercise.

Tonight's Exercise: Acting on the Dream Stage

You can use the following simple technique to influence your dream maker to create a dream based on your life's mission. The object is to have a dream that will shed light upon how your other self-segments feel about your conscious choice of a possible life's mission. This choice should resonate within all aspects of your being. Each part of yourself must be moving in the same direction, all committed to your life's mission. This will ensure your ultimate success as well as provide spiritual and emotional fulfillment.

Shortly before going to sleep repeat the following affirmation. It will set the tone for your dreams tonight.

> I am a _____ (state your vocation/
> occupation) . I wish to accomplish my life's mission by
> _____(this action). My dream tonight will
> illuminate my consciousness with the awareness
> of how my life's mission will unfold.

For example you may say: "I am a *healer.* I wish to accomplish my life's mission by *healing people with therapeutic massage.* My dream tonight will illuminate my consciousness with the awareness of how my life's mission will unfold."

Repeat this affirmation several times as you fall asleep. Your dreams will contain important messages from your soul self that will either affirm your choice of a life's mission or point you in a different direction.

Upon awakening in the morning, remember to lie still and keep your eyes closed. Focus your attention on accessing your dream memories. Take some time to allow your dream memories to impress themselves upon your waking mind. After a few minutes, record your dreams in your journal.

When you have finished, begin to unseal the messages hidden within your dreams. Call upon Archangel Gabriel to bring you insight as you interpret your dreams by saying the following prayer of invocation.

Dear Archangel Gabriel,
*   I ask that your messages be clear and your presence strong as*
I interpret my dreams today. I trust in your guidance and
accept your divine help. I commit myself to the process of per-
sonal growth and the accomplishment of my personal mission.
Amen.

Next, perform all seven steps of the interpretation process. The seven steps (from chapter 3) are repeated for you below:

1. Make an inventory or list of each of the characters that appear in your dream, both human and nonhuman.

2. Examine your feelings about the dream characters.

3. Examine your role in the dream and your relationships to the dream characters.

4. Review the actions taking place in the dream.

5. Find out what aspect of yourself the dream characters represent by engaging them in imaginary conversation.

6. Analyze the dream setting (location/time of day/environment).

7. Consider your current life situation.

You will know that you have arrived at the correct dream interpretation when you feel something "click" within you. Don't be discouraged if this doesn't happen right away. The message of your dream may become unsealed over the course of the day or it may take even more time to emerge as you work through your spiritual growth issues.

Meeting Archangel Uriel

For the past several nights Archangel Gabriel has led you on a journey to uncover your life's mission. It is now time to meet with Archangel Uriel in the dream worlds. Uriel's loving energy helps us rekindle the spirit of appreciation for life that we knew as little children, alive and present in the sacredness of each moment.

Archangel Uriel is one of the least depicted of the four archangels. Most images of him were removed from the Church several centuries ago for unknown reasons. The most common images that remain show Uriel carrying a scroll or a book in one hand with a small flame burning in the palm of his other hand. This flame signifies the undying love of the Creator that illuminates the world so that we may see the beauty in it and in ourselves. The flame also gives warmth, symbolizing the awareness of the heart aflame with the love of God.

Uriel helps us to be all that we are in each moment. For example, if you feel angry, allow yourself to accept this feeling and then try to understand what it is telling you about you or your situation. Don't tell yourself that you can't feel anger. Rather, ask yourself how you can constructively deal with what you feel. This very important response signifies that we have accepted our human nature and is akin to the age-old adage, "Man, know thyself."

Uriel reminds us that the end result of the process of angelic illumination is not to make us angels. Rather it is to help us to enhance our human experience and to live life—in truth, in joy, and in love—as the integrated spiritual/physical beings that we are.

Uriel shows us the state of simply *being*, the state where we accept, appreciate, and learn from each and every experience. Uriel's attributes are love, beauty, and awareness. His process is appreciation, and his power is being.

Uriel's Dream Message

The following text is from a channeling of Archangel Uriel on the topic of dreams.

I bring to you a message of appreciation. Appreciate your dream worlds. In them you can explore, create, learn, and grow in ways you are unable to consciously. You can more easily meet me in full consciousness during your dreams. When your physical body is asleep, the noise of your conscious day-to-day world is temporarily quieted. The quieting of your conscious mind helps you to perceive messages from the Angelic realms and your other self-segments. It is then that your conscious mind becomes directed to your inner worlds. And it is when you begin to hear your internal messages and experience the love and support of the angels that you can move to uncover the hidden meaning of those messages. My heart is composed of the love of God. As my heart is composed, yours is as well, for we are kin—created in God's image, endowed with the power of feeling, seeing, acting, and being. Reach out to me, and I will be with you. Call upon me and invoke my presence as you go to sleep, and I will petition the Lord to send grace and light into your consciousness so that you can more easily see and appreciate the full wonder and awe of life. I send my love to you, now and always.

—URIEL

Attuning Your Consciousness to the Guiding Angel

Uriel, archangel of love, beauty, and awareness, will be your guide tonight during your journey into the dream worlds. Before performing tonight's dream exercise, use the following invocation and contemplation to attune yourself to his holy presence.

Invocation to Archangel Uriel

> Uriel, holy angel of God,
>   Come to me tonight. May your peaceful presence lead me to a deeper appreciation of my dream worlds. Help me to understand and integrate all parts of myself so that I may live a life rooted in love and joy once again. Let my decisions be based on love, not fear; and let my every action contribute to the never-ending demonstration of the Creator's love for all life. Amen.

Allow yourself to feel Uriel's presence enter your heart. Next, to further attune your consciousness to the guiding presence for tonight, read and contemplate the following words.

Be not afraid to reveal your whole heart. As you speak, so
shall you grow, and so shall your relationships deepen.

—Archangel Uriel

Allow these words to wash over you. Rest with them for a few minutes and
feel your whole being come into alignment with their truth. Do this for a few
minutes. You have now opened a conduit to the wisdom radiating from the
author of tonight's contemplation—Archangel Uriel. Open your eyes and
continue tonight's session by performing the following dream exercise.

Tonight's Exercise: Meeting Archangel Uriel

Archangel Uriel wishes to meet with you in your dream worlds tonight. Uriel
is the archangel of love, beauty, and awareness. Often upon meeting him, one
becomes filled with appreciation of the eternal nature of the moment. To help
set the tone for meeting Uriel, relax and repeat the following affirmation several times directly before retiring.

> **I prepare my consciousness in purity to receive the blessings and
> message of the Creator as delivered by the holy Archangel Uriel.
> I invite him into my dream worlds tonight.**

As you repeat this affirmation, feel the presence of Archangel Uriel growing
stronger and closer. Continue to repeat the affirmation and gently relax into
a deep and restful sleep knowing that soon you will meet the personage or
some aspect of the glorious archangel of God, Uriel, in your dreams.

Upon awakening in the morning, remember to lie still and keep your eyes
closed. Focus your attention on accessing your dream memories. Take some
time to allow your dream memories to impress themselves upon your waking
mind. After a few minutes, record your dreams in your journal.

When you have finished, begin to unseal the messages hidden within your
dreams. Call upon Archangel Uriel to bring you insight as you interpret your
dreams by saying the following prayer of invocation.

> *Dear Archangel Uriel,*
> *Be with me now as I uncover the hidden meaning of my*
> *dreams. I invoke your joyful and loving presence. Help me to see*
> *and appreciate all the parts of myself that I meet within my*
> *dreams. Amen.*

Next, perform all seven steps of the interpretation process. The seven steps (from chapter 3) are repeated for you below:

1. Make an inventory or list of each of the characters that appear in your dream, both human and nonhuman.
2. Examine your feelings about the dream characters.
3. Examine your role in the dream and your relationships to the dream characters.
4. Review the actions taking place in the dream.
5. Find out what aspect of yourself the dream characters represent by engaging them in imaginary conversation.
6. Analyze the dream setting (location/time of day/environment).
7. Consider your current life situation.

You will know that you have arrived at the correct dream interpretation when you feel something "click" within you. Don't be discouraged if this doesn't happen right away. The message of your dream may become unsealed over the course of the day or it may take even more time to emerge as you work through your spiritual growth issues.

Life Review Dream

While we all know that we will not be on earth forever, we rarely focus on the time when we will no longer be here. Tonight you will learn how to use your dreams to show you what you need to do and how to live so that when you look back upon your life, you will be filled with a sense of self-worth and accomplishment. To do this you will focus on the direction your life is presently taking.

All of life's situations and forms are subject to and embedded within the continual flux of divine energy. Death, rebirth, and resurrection occur daily on many levels. This cycle extends from the micro cells that construct our physical body to the powerhouse that lights the universes of God. It is the divine movement of energy that we experience.

The whole world is an extension of God. What we see in the world around us is the result of a long thread of cause and effect traversing through the millennia. The world and everything in it—good and evil—is an expression of the totality of the life force as well as humanity's choices. Our most powerful ability as humans is our ability to choose.

The simple answer to the mystery of consciousness is that everything that we experience exists. The underlying questions that propel our growth and understanding are: (1) Why did we experience something? and (2) What predominant power or hidden cause triggered the experience to occur?

In order to gain the most from life, and to give the most to life, we must learn to appreciate the value of living in tune with our self-segments. Many times we are not even aware of our self-segments, their purposes, or their messages. Yet each part of our self defines our very humanity. Appreciation links these parts together, and this link forms a chain that connects us, one to the other, reflecting God's design for humanity.

An excellent way to deeply appreciate life is to contemplate the eventual experience that all who have been born on this earth will some day go through: the death of the physical body. As difficult as this subject is, we must have the courage to face it head-on. Accepting the eventual dissolution of our body needs to be more than merely a mental understanding.

For example, while we know we must pay our monthly bills, it is a distinctly different experience to actually sit down and write the checks. In the same way, death is simply a mental fact that we each know but do not truly understand until we are called upon to pay that final coin. Contemplating our body's eventual demise helps us to appreciate and value the gift of our consciousness.

Finding Meaning in Our Lives

Some people become discouraged by the fear that their efforts will go to waste. They then give up and become mired down by a sense of meaninglessness. Such people think, *If everything I create will someday decay, then what have I gained in the process of creation?* They forget that creation, like life itself, is a process. It is in the journey that we learn and grow.

For example, you don't go to the movie theater to see the end of a movie—you go to see the *complete story*—from beginning to end, and everything in between. In the same way, we don't come to Earth just to build something or to reach a particular state of awareness—we come for the total experience—from start to finish.

As a wave rushing to the shore reaches the beach, dissipates, and flows back into the ocean, we ride a wave of energy toward our goal. This energy takes us to the land of our creation. Then, like the wave that recedes into the ocean, our creation will eventually return to the One Energy to be renewed again and again. This is the eternal play of life. Those who accept it live in the moment, with awe, gratitude, and humility. For what we now know is only a small fraction of the universe.

Attuning Your Consciousness to the Guiding Angel

Uriel, archangel of love, beauty, and awareness, will be your guide tonight during your journey into the dream worlds. Before performing tonight's dream exercise, use the following invocation and contemplation to attune yourself to his holy presence.

Invocation to Archangel Uriel

> *Uriel, holy angel of God,*
> *Come to me tonight. May your peaceful presence lead me to a deeper appreciation of my dream worlds. Help me to understand and integrate all parts of myself so that I may live a life rooted in love and joy once again. Let my decisions be based on love, not fear; and let my every action contribute to the never-ending demonstration of the Creator's love for all life. Amen.*

Allow yourself to feel Uriel's presence enter your heart. Next, to further attune your consciousness to the guiding presence for tonight, read and contemplate the following words.

> Appreciate deeply and reflect on the absolute truth and beauty of yourself. At the same time appreciate your fellow-man's divergent inner perceptions and reality. For each perception is a layer of your ultimate reality.
>
> —Archangel Uriel

Allow these words to wash over you. Rest with them for a few minutes and feel your whole being come into alignment with their truth. Do this for a few minutes. You have now opened a conduit to the wisdom radiating from the author of tonight's contemplation—Archangel Uriel. Open your eyes and continue tonight's session by performing the following dream exercise.

Tonight's Exercise: Life Review Dream

Although life seems like it will never end, we know that our time on earth is temporary. As a visitor to a foreign land must return home, we too must each return to our true home someday. On that final day, we will have the opportunity to look back upon the scenes of our life—the accomplishments, the loves, and the regrets. This process is known as "The Life Review."

Tonight your dreams will highlight an aspect of your life that needs attention. The clues in this dream will give you the opportunity to correct the situation now, during this lifetime, so you don't find yourself in the afterlife unable to make amends. You may also have a dream that foreshadows the life review that, given your present direction and choices, you will likely experience.

Archangel Uriel will assist you in this process. Your life review dream will present important images and symbols. Based on what you learn in your dreams tonight, you may wish to make changes in your life. As you go to sleep tonight say the following prayer several times. It will set the tone for your dreams.

> *Dear Uriel,*
>   *Help me to view with courage and sensitivity the moments and events of my lifetime. Help me to review, understand, and appreciate my time upon this earth. Amen.*

As you repeat this prayer, feel the presence of Archangel Uriel growing stronger and closer. Continue to repeat the prayer and gently relax into a deep and restful sleep knowing that Archangel Uriel will guide you in your dreams tonight.

––––––––––

Upon awakening in the morning, remember to lie still and keep your eyes closed. Focus your attention on accessing your dream memories. Take some time to allow your dream memories to impress themselves upon your waking mind. After a few minutes, record your dreams in your journal.

When you have finished, begin to unseal the messages hidden within your dreams. Call upon Archangel Uriel to bring you insight as you interpret your dreams by saying the following prayer of invocation.

> *Dear Archangel Uriel,*
>   *Be with me now as I uncover the hidden meaning of my dreams. I invoke your joyful and loving presence to help me see and appreciate all the parts of myself that I meet within my dreams. Amen.*

Next, perform all seven steps of the interpretation process. The seven steps (from chapter 3) are repeated for you below:

1. Make an inventory or list of each of the characters that appear in your dream, both human and nonhuman.
2. Examine your feelings about the dream characters.
3. Examine your role in the dream and your relationships to the dream characters.
4. Review the actions taking place in the dream.
5. Find out what aspect of yourself the dream characters represent by engaging them in imaginary conversation.
6. Analyze the dream setting (location/time of day/environment).
7. Consider your current life situation.

You will know that you have arrived at the correct dream interpretation when you feel something "click" within you. Don't be discouraged if this doesn't happen right away. The message of your dream may become unsealed over the course of the day or it may take even more time to emerge as you work through your spiritual growth issues.

Meeting Your Guardian Angel

Your guardian angel was chosen especially for you from God's host of heavenly angels. Your angel has been charged with the mission to guide and protect you from the moment of your conception, throughout your life, in good times and in bad. He will never abandon you, not even in death; for it is he who will be your guiding light as you let go of the physical and move into the spiritual realms. You will have the opportunity to meet with this beautiful and important angel tonight in your dream worlds.

Guardian angels are first spoken of in the Bible in the book of Exodus 23:20–21, where God told Moses He would send an angel to guard him: "See, I am sending an angel before you, to guard you on the way and to bring you to the place I have prepared. Be attentive to him and heed his voice...for my name is in him."

The role of guardian angels is further clarified in Psalm 91:10–12: "There shall no evil befall thee, neither shall any affliction come nigh thy dwelling. For he shall give his angels charge over thee, to keep thee in all thy ways. They shall bear thee up in their hands, lest thou dash thy foot against a stone."

In the New Testament, Jesus referred to the guardian angels of little children. This subject arose when Jesus' disciples asked, "Who is of greatest importance in the kingdom of God?" Jesus answered them by talking about how important it is to become like the little child and to take good care of our children. In Matthew 18:3–5, Jesus said, "I assure you, unless you change and become like little children, you will not enter the kingdom of God....Whoever welcomes one such child for my sake welcomes me."

And, in Matthew 18:10, Jesus said, "See that you never despise one of these little ones. I assure you, *their angels* in heaven constantly behold my heavenly Father's face."

Your guardian angel was chosen with great care and love. For just as each human is unique and particularly qualified for a specific mission, so too is each angel a unique and wondrous creation of God, gifted with qualities and abilities that expand and grow as the angel evolves.

Guardian angels have inner qualities, virtues, and abilities that are important to the evolution of your soul. If you already have an impression of your
guardian angel, you have likely sensed your angel's inner qualities.

You can, in part, determine the personal attributes of your guardian angel by
meditating upon the personal qualities you have always wanted to increase
within yourself. For example, if you would like to increase your compassion and
your generosity, then your angel very likely possesses these qualities. Likewise, if
you have always wanted to improve your sense of humor, then your guardian
angel probably has a fine sense of humor, and he (or she) has been trying to
increase your awareness and sensitivity to the humor in your life. Remember,
God chose your particular angel for you because your angel's qualities and energies will help you build these same qualities and energies within you.

Attuning Your Consciousness to the Guiding Angel

Uriel, archangel of love, beauty, and awareness, will be your guide tonight
during your journey into the dream worlds. Before performing tonight's
dream exercise, use the following invocation and contemplation to attune
yourself to his holy presence.

Invocation to Archangel Uriel

> *Uriel, holy angel of God,*
>   *Come to me tonight. May your peaceful presence lead me to a*
> *deeper appreciation of my dream worlds. Help me to under-*
> *stand and integrate all parts of myself so that I may live a life*
> *rooted in love and joy once again. Let my decisions be based on*
> *love, not fear; and let my every action contribute to the never-*
> *ending demonstration of the Creator's love for all life. Amen.*

Allow yourself to feel Uriel's presence enter your heart. Next, to further
attune your consciousness to the guiding presence for tonight, read and contemplate the following words.

> We are invisible to the eyes of the body but are not hidden
> to the soul who moves in truth; to one who allows divine
> energy to move through the centers of their being because
> they have learned how to process their experiences.
>
>   —ARCHANGEL URIEL

Allow these words to wash over you. Rest with them for a few minutes and
feel your whole being come into alignment with their truth. Do this for a few

minutes. You have now opened a conduit to the wisdom radiating from the author of tonight's contemplation—Archangel Uriel. Open your eyes and continue tonight's session by performing the following dream exercise.

Tonight's Exercise: Meeting Your Guardian Angel

We each have a special guardian angel who watches out for us in our daily life. But did you know that your guardian angel also helps you in your dream worlds? While guardian angels usually assist beneath the level of conscious awareness, you can actually have the wonderful experience of meeting your angel face to face in your dreams. Tonight is a good night to do just that.

Before going to sleep, close your eyes and think about your guardian angel. Imagine yourself enfolded in the love of this beautiful being. Breathe in and out slowly as you focus on each of the following gifts your guardian angel graciously provides for you each day of your life: *devotion, protection, support, encouragement, guidance, inspiration, a lifetime of unconditional love.*

Allow your heart to expand in thanksgiving. Stay in this place of thanksgiving for several minutes.

Then gently relax as you say the following prayer.

> *Dear Guardian Angel, my protector and guide,*
> *I desire to meet with you in my dreams tonight. I ask that*
> *you help me to see your beautiful form. Lend me your wisdom*
> *and advice as it applies to the issues of my life. Amen.*

As you repeat this prayer, feel the presence of your guardian angel growing stronger and closer. Continue to repeat the prayer and gently relax into a deep and restful sleep, knowing that soon you will meet the personage or some aspect of your guardian angel in your dreams.

Upon awakening in the morning, remember to lie still and keep your eyes closed. Focus your attention on accessing your dream memories. Take some time to allow your dream memories to impress themselves upon your waking mind. After a few minutes, record your dreams in your journal.

When you have finished, begin to unseal the messages hidden within your dreams. Call upon Archangel Uriel to bring you insight as you interpret your dreams by saying the following prayer of invocation.

Dear Archangel Uriel,

Be with me now as I uncover the hidden meaning of my dreams. I invoke your joyful and loving presence to help me see and appreciate all that my dream worlds have revealed to me. Amen.

Next, perform all seven steps of the interpretation process. The seven steps (from chapter 3) are repeated for you below:

1. Make an inventory or list of each of the characters that appear in your dream, both human and nonhuman.
2. Examine your feelings about the dream characters.
3. Examine your role in the dream and your relationships to the dream characters.
4. Review the actions taking place in the dream.
5. Find out what aspect of yourself the dream characters represent by engaging them in imaginary conversation.
6. Analyze the dream setting (location/time of day/environment).
7. Consider your current life situation.

You will know that you have arrived at the correct dream interpretation when you feel something "click" within you. Don't be discouraged if this doesn't happen right away. The message of your dream may become unsealed over the course of the day or it may take even more time to emerge as you work through your spiritual growth issues.

Messages from Your Soul Self

As you have learned, your soul is the key component of the self. It is imperishable, composed of pure Spirit. Given life by the Creator, the soul extends itself into the worlds of energy, matter, space, and time in order to gain the experience by which it can grow and expand. Tonight you will learn how you, as the conscious self, can connect with the wisdom and direction of your soul. This will help you fulfill your soul's plan and purpose for this lifetime.

Of all the self-segments that we can connect with in our dreams, the soul self is the most important because the blueprint and plan for our current lifetime resides within it. Our body has been spun into existence via the energy impulses of our soul. Therefore, while we are integrating our other self-segments (the basic/subconscious self and the emotional self), we should also strive to gain a clear and direct connection with our soul. This will give us access to the wisdom stored in the other esoteric component of the self called the higher self.

Each night as we enter sleep we are born into a new world, gain experience there, and then return hours later to the waking state. This progression is a mini-cycle that mirrors the three main stages of life: the birth into human consciousness; the experience of the human consciousness in this world; and the death of the human vehicle and the subsequent transition back into the spiritual/nonphysical state. Each transition is an experience that consists of the movement of energy into and out of different forms—all for the benefit of our growth and awareness.

For example, a container such as a glass full of water is actually holding matter in a certain formation. The purpose of the glass in this case is to hold energy in a form that allows us to consume it and then transmute it into other forms for survival. This formation is temporary. If the glass tips over, the water will spill, changing its shape. Depending upon the temperature in the room, the water could evaporate into the air.

In a similar way, dreams are containers for ethereal energy to fill. Shapes and forms are filled out into three-dimensional modalities with lightning speed by the master artist of our combined self-segments. As with all artists, creativity is born of a desire to move energy from one state to another. It is, in part, the soul's emulation of the divine impulse of the Creator that moves us to create and manifest in our world.

These pages, upon which the ink is printed, are in essence yet another container for energy, enabling it to be transformed for the purpose of communication. Communication strengthens bonds by solidifying the energy patterns between two points. The communication that occurs in your dreams has the same basic purpose—to solidify your whole being into one finely tuned vehicle for conscious experience in this world and all the worlds of God.

In order to determine our life's mission we need to connect to the soul self. This is essential if we are to understand and complete our mission here on earth. We can bring forth knowledge and direction from our soul into our conscious mind by interpreting the messages that the soul extends to us in our dreams.

The stronger your connection with your soul, the more clearly and frequently you will receive its messages of guidance and support. Your conscious choice to connect to your soul self in your dreams is the beginning of a long and beneficial relationship with your soul—your connection to the divine consciousness.

Attuning Your Consciousness to the Guiding Angel

Uriel, archangel of love, beauty, and awareness, will be your guide tonight during your journey into the dream worlds. Before performing tonight's dream exercise, use the following invocation and contemplation to attune yourself to his holy presence.

Invocation to Archangel Uriel

> Uriel, holy angel of God,
>   Come to me tonight. May your peaceful presence lead me to a deeper appreciation of my dream worlds. Help me to understand and integrate all parts of myself so that I may live a life rooted in love and joy once again. Let my decisions be based on love, not fear; and let my every action contribute to the neverending demonstration of the Creator's love for all life. Amen.

Allow yourself to feel Uriel's presence enter your heart. Next, to further attune your consciousness to the guiding presence for tonight, read and contemplate the following words.

> From deep within stirs the voice of the conscience until the whispering of the soul self becomes like a trumpet heralding

the dawn of a new day of consciousness—imbued with the
desire to grow, to accept, and to learn.

—ARCHANGEL URIEL

Allow these words to wash over you. Rest with them for a few minutes and
feel your whole being come into alignment with their truth. Do this for a few
minutes. You have now opened a conduit to the wisdom radiating from the
author of tonight's contemplation—Archangel Uriel. Open your eyes and
continue tonight's session by performing the following dream exercise.

Tonight's Exercise: Connecting with Your Soul Self

Your soul self wishes to communicate with you in your dream worlds. Your
soul is the indestructible part of you that is in contact with divine energy at all
times. The knowledge of your past (and probable future) is always available to
your soul—including the blueprint for your present lifetime. You can prepare
to receive its direct messages in your dreams by performing the following
technique.

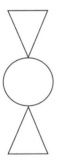

1. Relax and close your eyes. Next, imagine a pyramid
   shape floating in front of you. The pyramid represents
   your basic self and your emotional self. At the apex of
   the pyramid is a sphere. This sphere represents your
   conscious self. Directly above the sphere you see
   another, inverted pyramid. Its inverted point sits
   directly on top of the sphere. The inverted pyramid
   represents your higher and soul selves.

2. Watch as the inverted pyramid begins to fill with a
   golden liquid. As the golden energy fills the pyramid,
   allow yourself to consciously open to and accept this
golden energy within you. As you do, the golden liquid begins to leave
the inverted pyramid and enter the sphere. This continues until the
golden essence has entirely filled the sphere. This essence represents
the messages of your soul, which you have accepted into your conscious mind. Continue to visualize this golden energy as you drift off
to sleep.

This technique will stimulate a dream that contains messages from your soul.
By studying these messages you can determine how well you are understanding and fulfilling your soul's plan for this life.

———————

Upon awakening in the morning, remember to lie still and keep your eyes closed. Focus your attention on accessing your dream memories. Take some time to allow your dream memories to impress themselves upon your waking mind. After a few minutes, record your dreams in your journal.

When you have finished, begin to unseal the messages hidden within your dreams. Call upon Archangel Uriel to bring you insight as you interpret your dreams by saying the following prayer of invocation.

> *Dear Archangel Uriel,*
> *Be with me now as I uncover the hidden meaning of my dreams. I invoke your joyful and loving presence. Help me to see and appreciate all the parts of myself that I meet within my dreams. Amen.*

Next, perform all seven steps of the interpretation process. The seven steps (from chapter 3) are repeated for you below:

1. Make an inventory or list of each of the characters that appear in your dream, both human and nonhuman.
2. Examine your feelings about the dream characters.
3. Examine your role in the dream and your relationships to the dream characters.
4. Review the actions taking place in the dream.
5. Find out what aspect of yourself the dream characters represent by engaging them in imaginary conversation.
6. Analyze the dream setting (location/time of day/environment).
7. Consider your current life situation.

You will know that you have arrived at the correct dream interpretation when you feel something "click" within you. Don't be discouraged if this doesn't happen right away. The message of your dream may become unsealed over the course of the day or it may take even more time to emerge as you work through your spiritual growth issues.

The Archangels' Chakra-Balancing Dream

You have spent several nights journeying in the dream worlds with each of the archangels. You are now familiar with the presence, purpose, and energy streams that surround these holy messengers of God. Armed with this knowledge and experience, you are ready to move on to advanced dream topics. Tonight you will call upon the energies of each of the four archangels, as Raphael, archangel of healing, wholeness, and acceptance, leads you toward an understanding and balancing of your seven chakras in the dream worlds.

Everything in our universe is made manifest through the divine movement and energy of the Creator. Just as blood is the major component of our physical bodies, energy is the major component of the Creator's universal body, of which we are all a part. The same energy that created the particles of the universe has created our mortal bodies.

Our bodies receive and transmit energy. Within our mortal bodies lie other bodies of a higher vibration known as the inner bodies. Energy is shared between our physical body and our inner bodies through circular energy centers. Energy moves through these portals, causing them to spin in clockwise or counterclockwise directions.

These energy centers are also known as chakras. The word *chakra* comes from the Sanskrit *cakram*, or "circle/wheel." Hence the circular design of the energy centers. Within the human system there are seven main chakras. Each has a purpose, a color vibration, and a main function. As with the organs of the physical body, if one chakra is out of alignment it affects the whole system.

The seven chakras, the areas of the body they correspond to, their main colors, and their purposes are shown in the following chart.

Chakra	Location	Color	Purpose
crown	top of head	purple	receive divine energy
third eye	between eyebrows	indigo	channel the will energy
throat	throat	blue	merge the will and heart
heart	heart	green	transmute love energy
solar plexus	stomach	yellow	feeling energy
sexual	genitals	orange	creative energy
base	base of spine	red	grounding earth energy

In addition to the seven main chakras, the human system contains hundreds of smaller energy points. These additional energy points are similar to the energy meridians used in acupuncture. Rather than work with these small ancillary centers, we focus on the seven main centers during our energy work and healing meditations. Regulating the flows of the larger centers has a more immediate effect upon our general well-being and balance.

You can modify the flow of energy to and from each chakra by directly focusing upon that chakra. The following chart shows which archangel works most directly with each major energy center. Focusing on the archangel corresponding to the chakra center in your prayers, healing sessions, or meditations can help regulate the flow of energy in and out of that center, bringing healing and wholeness to the spiritual/physical body system.

Archangel	Chakra	Power
Michael	crown, third eye, throat	seeing
Raphael	throat, heart, solar plexus	expressing
Gabriel	crown, sexual, base	acting
Uriel	third eye, heart, sexual	being

You can call upon an archangel's energy and presence by simply focusing your attention on a specific energy center. Such focus brings you into harmonic alignment with the key energy flows of the archangels. Then you can proceed to communicate with them through intuitive channels, such as inner dialoging and verbal or written channeling. While outward manifestations are possible, the angels generally use inner methods, particularly the dream state, to reach us. Their appearance in the dream state and during meditation is much less of a shock to our system than a sudden waking-world visitation.

This is not to say that direct visitations with the angels are not possible, rather that it is easier to prepare and meet the angels in other ways. One must be pure of heart to receive the visitation of the angels. If you are pure of heart, you will be able to receive them in the inner worlds and may even be fortunate enough to experience them in full waking consciousness. Many saints whose hearts were pure reported receiving direct visitations and communications from the angels while fully awake.

Attuning Your Consciousness to the Guiding Angel

Raphael, archangel of healing, wholeness, and acceptance, will be your guide tonight during your journey into the dream worlds. Before performing tonight's dream exercise, use the following invocation and contemplation to attune yourself to his holy presence.

Invocation to Archangel Raphael

> *Raphael, holy angel of God,*
> *I desire to know your healing presence. I have made a place*
> *in my heart for your visitation. Come to me in my dreams*
> *tonight and share with me your wisdom and love as I move to*
> *express my innermost thoughts and feelings. I desire to know*
> *God and to love myself again. Raphael, help me to express and*
> *then heal my pain. I await you in hopeful anticipation of your*
> *radiant presence. Amen.*

Allow yourself to feel Raphael's presence enter your heart. Next, to further attune your consciousness to the guiding presence for tonight, read and contemplate the following words.

> In your heart lies the truth—hidden behind walls of fear. I
> and the other archangels send our love to you to empower
> you to help yourself heal and grow in the Lord.
>
> —Archangel Raphael

Allow these words to wash over you. Rest with them for a few minutes and feel your whole being come into alignment with their truth. Do this for a few minutes. You have now opened a conduit to the wisdom radiating from the author of tonight's contemplation—Archangel Raphael. Open your eyes and continue tonight's session by performing the following dream exercise.

Tonight's Exercise: The Archangels' Chakra-Balancing Dream

The four archangels, led by Archangel Raphael, will perform a chakra balancing upon your inner bodies. This will happen within your dream worlds. You may or may not recall the dream in which the healing was performed, but upon awakening you should sense a more balanced feeling or a new sense of strength. To invite the archangels and their energy into your dreams perform the following.

1. Upon retiring for sleep, relax and close your eyes. Imagine a golden light entering you. It travels from the top of your head down to your feet and back toward your head. Continue to relax as the cycle begins again. As the balancing energy pulses through you, it passes through each chakra from the crown chakra at the top of your head to the base chakra at the base of your spine.

2. After bathing in this beautiful pulsing light, repeat the following prayer several times.

> *Dear Michael, Raphael, Gabriel, and Uriel,*
> *I invite you into my dreams tonight. I am prepared to receive your healing energies. I thank you now for your love, protection, and care as I strive to become more balanced in all ways. Amen.*

Continue to imagine the healing energy of God pulsing through you as you repeat this prayer while allowing yourself to move along with the golden light. Release your consciousness to the guidance of your dream maker and the four archangels. Gently relax and fall into a deep restful sleep.

———————

Upon awakening in the morning, remember to lie still and keep your eyes closed. Focus your attention on accessing your dream memories. Take some time to allow your dream memories to impress themselves upon your waking mind. After a few minutes, record your dreams in your journal.

When you have finished, begin to unseal the messages hidden within your dreams. Call upon Archangel Raphael to bring you insight as you interpret your dreams by saying the following prayer of invocation.

> *Dear Archangel Raphael,*
> *Please send your healing light to illuminate my consciousness that I might better understand the communications sent to me in my dreams. Amen.*

Next, perform all seven steps of the interpretation process. The seven steps (from chapter 3) are repeated for you below:

1. Make an inventory or list of each of the characters that appear in your dream, both human and nonhuman.
2. Examine your feelings about the dream characters.
3. Examine your role in the dream and your relationships to the dream characters.
4. Review the actions taking place in the dream.
5. Find out what aspect of yourself the dream characters represent by engaging them in imaginary conversation.
6. Analyze the dream setting (location/time of day/environment).
7. Consider your current life situation.

You will know that you have arrived at the correct dream interpretation when you feel something "click" within you. Don't be discouraged if this doesn't happen right away. The message of your dream may become unsealed over the course of the day or it may take even more time to emerge as you work through your spiritual growth issues.

Pearls of Wisdom Dream

Tonight you will learn to access your pearls of wisdom by journeying into the dream worlds with Archangel Michael. Pearls of wisdom are the knowledge and wisdom your soul has gained from all of its processed and integrated experiences, gathered over the course of multiple lifetimes on the earth plane. Tonight you will communicate with your higher self, which stores your pearls of wisdom. We will also discuss past life regressions and spiritual readings, as they, too, can serve as portals to your wisdom pool.

Think, for a moment, about your experiences so far in this lifetime. What lessons have you learned? What knowledge have you accumulated from school, workshops, and seminars? Consider the various jobs you have had in your life. Like most people, you have probably held a variety of positions, each of which required a specific set of skills.

As you think about these things you can see that, as the physical embodiment of soul, you have gathered a vast amount of knowledge and skills in just this one lifetime. Can you imagine the resources you could access if you tapped into the distilled wisdom of *all* of your lifetimes? Well you can—because nothing you have learned is ever lost! It is held safe for you, in the repository of your higher self.

Your higher self contains the distilled knowledge and wisdom of all of your soul's experiences. You can access your pearls of wisdom through several different methods, including past-life regressions, spiritual readings, and dream study techniques—such as the one you will practice in tonight's exercise.

The methods listed above vary somewhat in purpose. Understanding their differences will help you to decide which method to use at any particular time.

The primary purpose of a past-life regression is to heal painful memories from your past lives so they do not negatively affect your present life. These memories are often caused by traumatic events, overwhelming losses, or difficult relationship issues that you could not resolve during a past lifetime. This is called emotional residue. You carry this residue with you from lifetime to lifetime until you get the opportunity to dissolve it by healing the associated memories.

We highly recommend that you call upon the angels, Jesus, or the saints to attend you during a past-life regression just as you do in your dream explorations. For example, Linda calls upon both Archangel Michael and Archangel Raphael to be her spiritual attendants during regressions. Michael helps her feel protected during the opening of her psychic wounds. Michael also uses his Sword of Truth during regressions to help Linda examine and understand the truth of her past experiences.

Raphael and his host of healing angels attend Linda's regressions to oversee the healing of her past-life wounds. Raphael helps Linda heal and release the emotional shock that surrounds her traumatic memories. Then Raphael and his healing angels "fill and seal" the psychic wounds with the light of God. At the end of the healing process—while Linda is bathed in the light of God and in communion with her higher self and her soul self—Archangel Michael steps in to help her recognize and retrieve the pearls of wisdom from that lifetime.

You can see that the healing that occurs during a past-life regression helps to make us whole. From this point of wholeness we can more easily access our stored wisdom to use in this life. We can also tap into strengths and skills that we developed in past lifetimes.

The main purpose of a spiritual reading is to promote healing by providing hope, encouragement, and spiritual direction. A good spiritual reader can help us deal with current life situations, relationship difficulties, and emotional conflicts. Even though readers often tap into past-life experiences, their primary focus is on the present life, especially in regard to helping the client recognize new opportunities for growth and creative expansion.

Finally, our dream worlds present us with many opportunities for the healing that is required to retrieve our pearls of wisdom. Our dream maker stimulates healing, wholeness, and creativity within each of our bodies (mental, physical, spiritual, emotional). It is not limited to a specific time frame, nor is it limited by physical laws or dimensions.

Regressions, readings, and dreams all bring us an awareness of our self-limiting blocks and patterns. Each method can be used effectively to heal and dissolve these blocks. But only one of these methods—dream study—is suited for use each night, at your own direction and at your own pace.

In tonight's dream journey Archangel Michael will help you to connect with the wisdom of your higher self. This connection is greatly enhanced by prayer work. Your prayers do not need to be lengthy or complicated. A daily simple prayer, like, "Dear God, shine the light of your love into my heart today," is enough. Allow your whole being to feel the simple honesty of these words. Prayer purifies you by dispelling the fears that cloud your consciousness.

As you clear these fears away you create a space for the light of God to enter you, in answer to your prayer.

Filled with light and free of fear, you can feel Michael's light calling you into the dream worlds where the wisdom of your higher self awaits you. Michael will help you find your pearls of wisdom—and he will help you carry these treasures back home to the purified consciousness of your waking mind.

Attuning Your Consciousness to the Guiding Angel

Michael, chief of the archangels, will be your guide tonight during your journey into the dream worlds. Before performing tonight's dream exercise, use the following invocation and contemplation to attune yourself to his holy presence.

Invocation to Archangel Michael

> *Michael, holy angel of God,*
>   *I invite you into my dream worlds and into my consciousness.*
> *I seek to uncover and understand the truth of my choices and to*
> *accept the results of all that I have put into action. Please help*
> *me to see myself more clearly and lend me the wisdom of your*
> *words and presence as I move to lift the Chalice of Justice and*
> *wield the Sword of Truth. Amen.*

Allow yourself to feel Michael's presence enter your heart. Next, to further attune your consciousness to the guiding presence for tonight, read and contemplate the following words.

> A divine gift of the Holy Spirit—the treasures from your
> own past—are being held safe for you by your higher self.
> Study your dream worlds, for that is where your treasures can
> be accessed.
>
> —ARCHANGEL MICHAEL

Allow these words to wash over you. Rest with them for a few minutes and feel your whole being come into alignment with their truth. Do this for a few minutes. You have now opened a conduit to the wisdom radiating from the author of tonight's contemplation—Archangel Michael. Open your eyes and continue tonight's session by performing the following dream exercise.

Tonight's Exercise: Pearls of Wisdom Dream

You can access your pearls of wisdom in the dream worlds tonight. The wisdom stored within you consists of the fully processed and integrated experiences of your past. Just as Jesus said, "Ask and you shall receive," you can ask your own higher self any question you wish and you will receive an answer.

Michael is the archangel who helps us locate and connect with the wisdom stored in our higher self. He also helps us to navigate and explore our past lives during regressions and within the dream worlds—if we call upon him for assistance.

To begin this technique, light a blue candle to signify the truth that is Michael. Recite the following prayer. Feel the intention of the words resonate within your heart.

A Prayer for Wisdom

> O Radiant Michael, holy messenger of God,
>   Let thy light shine ever before me as I search for the wisdom
> that was once mine, lifetimes ago. Be a beacon pointing to the
> repository of my higher self, wherein lie the treasures of my soul
> amid the lessons of uncounted lifetimes. Thank you for showing me
> the way to these gifts, Michael, and thank God, our Father, for
> holding these treasures safe for me within the light of His love,
> that I might reclaim that which I thought I had lost. May I
> always use my gifts in loving service to God and humanity. Amen.

As you go to sleep tonight, think of the most important question you wish to ask your higher self. Repeat the following request.

I desire to connect to the wisdom within me. I wish to know
_____ **(state your question or concern).**

Repeat this request several times as you drift off to sleep. You can feel Michael's radiant presence relax and comfort you as you gently move into the dream worlds.

———————

Upon awakening in the morning, remember to lie still and keep your eyes closed. Focus your attention on accessing your dream memories. Take some time to allow your dream memories to impress themselves upon your waking mind. After a few minutes, record your dreams in your journal.

When you have finished, begin to unseal the messages hidden within your dreams. Call upon Archangel Michael to bring you insight as you interpret your dreams by saying the following prayer of invocation.

> *Dear Archangel Michael,*
>   *Please shine your light of truth upon my dream messages.*
> *Help me to unseal their wisdom so that I might better under-*
> *stand myself, my relationships, and my mission for this lifetime.*
> *Amen.*

Next, perform all seven steps of the interpretation process. The seven steps (from chapter 3) are repeated for you below:

1. Make an inventory or list of each of the characters that appear in your dream, both human and nonhuman.
2. Examine your feelings about the dream characters.
3. Examine your role in the dream and your relationships to the dream characters.
4. Review the actions taking place in the dream.
5. Find out what aspect of yourself the dream characters represent by engaging them in imaginary conversation.
6. Analyze the dream setting (location/time of day/environment).
7. Consider your current life situation.

You will know that you have arrived at the correct dream interpretation when you feel something "click" within you. Don't be discouraged if this doesn't happen right away. The message of your dream may become unsealed over the course of the day or it may take even more time to emerge as you work through your spiritual growth issues.

DAY 23

Ask, and It Shall Be Given

Just as Jesus said, "Ask, and it shall be given," you can ask your dream maker to speak to you in a literal fashion, using your waking-world language rather than the symbols it usually employs. Archangel Raphael will be at your side, enhancing your communication with each part of yourself as you use the twin tools of imagination and belief in tonight's session.

Imagine having a dream where your dream maker presents vital pieces of information to you in a clear and direct manner. It may sound odd and perhaps a bit against the grain to believe that you can ask your other self-segments to communicate with you in your waking-world language. But this can be accomplished by the strength of your belief and perseverance. Your self-segments will strive to speak your language if you let them know how important it is.

For example, you may have a dream in which you receive a letter that gives you specific instructions, insights, or messages from your soul self. This direct message might be spoken to you by a character in your dream. In this type of dream you would not have to guess at the dream's message. You would only need to read or listen and interpret the words as you would a waking-world communication. Ask yourself the following questions: Who is the message from? What is the purpose of the message? What action or actions (if any) should I take in light of the message?

Our dreams normally speak to us in a rich, symbolic language because that is the natural language of our subconscious, just as it is the language of humanity's collective subconscious. The saying, "one picture is worth a thousand words," helps us to understand how our richly detailed dream language is actually a gift to us. Our dreams can communicate multiple layers of information in one single image. Thus, to get the most out of our dream messages, we must learn the beautiful and intricate language of our dreams.

However, sometimes we have a specific question that we would like a simple answer to. At these times we can ask our dream maker to answer our question in a clear, literal way. Keep in mind that because this is *not* the natural language of your dream maker the information you get will be somewhat limited. The best way to get a full, complete answer from your dream maker is to allow it to speak to you in its naturally symbolic language. Nevertheless, communication is a two-way street. Don't be surprised when you receive a literal answer to your question in your waking-world language.

Linda had the following dream after spending an evening with a friend discussing spirituality and the importance of being in the present moment. That night Linda asked her dream maker to send her a clear, easy to understand message about her spiritual life.

THE ILLUMINATION

I dreamed I was in Uncle Leo's house. I noticed flashes of lightning and heard thunder as I looked out the window. I realized this storm was an outward manifestation of my inner state (excitement and fear)—because somehow I could feel God approaching me. I was in a state of awe—honored to be having this incredible experience of God. Then I heard a voice speak the following words: "This is a special message from Dorothy. Your prayers are being answered." These words appeared simultaneously on a large screen to my left, in huge capital letters. At this point in the dream I remember wondering if I was worthy of this incredible experience and which of my prayers were being answered.

Then the illumination began—the drawing in of God's presence. I could feel Him as light throughout my body. It flashed into my awareness that three of my prayers were being answered: (1) Let me be aware of God's presence in each moment of my life; (2) Let me know God's will for me; (3) Let me accept God's will for me.

Then a second period of illumination occurred. Again I felt the drawing in of God's light and presence. After this I woke up with the song "Let there be peace on earth and let it begin with me," being sung within me—flowing and resonating through every part of my being.

Linda treasures this dream—especially the message imparted to her from her Aunt Dorothy (who had died several years earlier). Dorothy has appeared in several of Linda's dreams—always bearing messages and insights from the spiritual realms.

Imagination and Belief

Two simple tools will assist you when you ask your self-segments to communicate in your language. Both require some effort on your part to use. The first is *belief.* When we choose to believe something, we open the window to a new experience—we have faith that something is possible.

The second tool is the *imagination.* With imagination we can see the impossible become reality. By seeing (in our mind's eye) the situation we wish to manifest, we create the inner form (container) for the energy of God to fill. There is nothing magical or unexplainable about this process. Yet this process fills us with awe and wonder at the infinite details of God's creation.

Attuning Your Consciousness to the Guiding Angel

Raphael, archangel of healing, wholeness, and acceptance, will be your guide tonight during your journey into the dream worlds. Before performing tonight's dream exercise, use the following invocation and contemplation to attune yourself to his holy presence.

Invocation to Archangel Raphael

> Raphael, holy angel of God,
>   I desire to know your healing presence. I have made a place
> in my heart for your visitation. Come to me in my dreams
> tonight and share with me your wisdom and love as I move to
> understand and communicate with each part of myself. I desire
> to know God and to love myself again. I await you in hopeful
> anticipation of your radiant presence. Amen.

Allow yourself to feel Raphael's presence enter your heart. Next, to further attune your consciousness to the guiding presence for tonight, read and contemplate the following words.

> Hearken to your dreams, for therein the Lord hath sealed
> his wisdom.
>
> —ARCHANGEL RAPHAEL

Allow these words to wash over you. Rest with them for a few minutes and feel your whole being come into alignment with their truth. Do this for a few minutes. You have now opened a conduit to the wisdom radiating from the author of tonight's contemplation—Archangel Raphael. Open your eyes and continue tonight's session by performing the following dream exercise.

Tonight's Exercise: Ask, and It Shall Be Given

In the following exercise you'll engage your imagination to help strengthen your belief that your dream maker can communicate with you using your waking language. This technique consists of two parts. The first part works with your imaginative abilities and the second involves using an affirmation to strengthen your belief that you can receive direct and clear communications from your dream maker.

Part 1

1. Relax and gently focus upon your mind's eye.
2. Imagine that you are dreaming. See yourself alone in a room. In that room you notice a table with an unopened letter on it. You pick up the letter and read the front of the envelope. Your name is clearly written in capital letters.
3. Open the envelope and pull out a single sheet of white paper. As you unfold the paper, you can see that there is a message on it, written in your native language. It is addressed to you and signed by a part of yourself.
4. Imagine reading the letter and understanding it fully. After a short time open your eyes.

The key to this exercise is to connect to the feeling of possibility. Performing this exercise will help your conscious self open to the experience of clear direct dream communication. It will stimulate your emotional and other self-segments to believe in this possibility as well.

Part 2

The second part of tonight's exercise involves asking your self-segments to communicate in your waking language. Send this message in the form of a positive affirmation. This is best done immediately before falling asleep.

The affirmation that you repeat in this part of the exercise must be infused with a strong and personal desire from your heart. A direct message that contains a high concentration of emotional energy will be more likely to get the attention of your other self-segments than one simply repeated by rote.

Why is this? Just take a look at how your conscious mind listens to outer-world sources. Someone who speaks quietly or with little passion is not likely to get your attention. But one who speaks with passion from his or her convictions will command your attention and focus. The same is true of your self-segments. They will respond better to your directives and affirmations when you send them strong messages imbued with passion and energy.

Dream Communication Affirmation

First make sure you generate a strong energy pool by focusing on an important concern or question. When you feel the energy within your heart, repeat the following affirmation several times as you go to sleep.

> **My dream self will send me a clear spoken or written message**
> **about _____ (state your concern) tonight.**

Use this technique only when you have an uncomplicated question that lends itself to being answered in a literal way. Remember, you will learn the most from your dream worlds by continuing to learn its mysterious language—the rich, symbolic natural voice of your dream self.

———————

Upon awakening in the morning, remember to lie still and keep your eyes closed. Focus your attention on accessing your dream memories. Take some time to allow your dream memories to impress themselves upon your waking mind. After a few minutes, record your dreams in your journal.

When you have finished, begin to unseal the messages hidden within your dreams. Call upon Archangel Raphael to bring you insight as you interpret your dreams by saying the following prayer of invocation.

> *Dear Archangel Raphael,*
>   *Please send your healing light to illuminate my consciousness*
> *that I might better understand the communications sent to me*
> *in my dreams. Amen.*

Next, perform all seven steps of the interpretation process. The seven steps (from chapter 3) are repeated for you below:

1. Make an inventory or list of each of the characters that appear in your dream, both human and nonhuman.
2. Examine your feelings about the dream characters.
3. Examine your role in the dream and your relationships to the dream characters.
4. Review the actions taking place in the dream.

5. Find out what aspect of yourself the dream characters represent by engaging them in imaginary conversation.

6. Analyze the dream setting (location/time of day/environment).

7. Consider your current life situation.

You will know that you have arrived at the correct dream interpretation when you feel something "click" within you. Don't be discouraged if this doesn't happen right away. The message of your dream may become unsealed over the course of the day or it may take even more time to emerge as you work through your spiritual growth issues.

DAY 24

Meeting Your Spirit Guides

Tonight you will learn about your spirit guides—who they are and how they can help you. You'll also learn the difference between spirit guides and angels. Tonight's dream session includes a technique for inviting your spirit guides to meet with you in the dream worlds.

Your spirit guides are nonphysical, spiritual beings from the invisible worlds that may or may not have once incarnated on the earth plane. Like attracts like; if they have experienced human lifetimes, often they will be someone you have known or worked with in a former incarnation. In such cases the spirit guides usually care deeply about you and have made a commitment to help you accomplish a particular goal in this lifetime.

Spirit guides often have specialized knowledge on a specific subject that they wish to share with you to help you accomplish an important goal or even your life's mission. You may have previously made an agreement with them, at the soul level, to accomplish a particular goal that will benefit both you and humanity.

How do angels and spirit guides differ? First of all, angels are beings of pure spirit. Their uppermost purpose and mission is to serve as messengers of God. They love and serve humanity by carrying our prayers and petitions to the throne of God—just as they choose to serve God by relaying His messages and instructions back to us. Angels usually use the dream worlds to relay messages to us; however at rare times the pure of heart have met them in visions while praying, during their meditations, or in waking-world visitations.

Spirit guides are often part of the human evolution and are more personality-based than the angels. Their interest and focus is much more concentrated on a specific area of learning that happens to coincide with your interests, studies, and goals.

The angels and the archangels exist in a parallel evolution to humanity. They are the builders of form and hold the matrices of energy for all life forms on Earth. The archangels sit at the top of the angelic hierarchy; because of this responsibility, they are very concerned with building unity between all life forms and the Creator. They work hand in hand with humanity, inspiring us to create as they build and hold together the energy matrices for the earth, for humanity, and for the Creator.

Some spirit guides originate from distant galaxies or star systems and have never incarnated on earth. But no matter what their origin, their purpose is to encourage and assist us in our daily lives—in personal growth issues, in our work endeavors, and in planetary concerns.

Remember that the spiritual beings of light and love (i.e., angels, spirit guides) *always* have positive, healing, and uplifting messages for you. If a negative, destructive, or obviously flattering message seems to come through in your dreams, it is either a hurt part of yourself trying to make itself known or a discarnate, earthbound entity masquerading as a light being.

In the latter case, simply spend more time cleansing your sleep/meditation space and invoking the white light of God by using the technique given to you on day 1 of your journey. It also helps to call upon the protective energy of Archangel Michael, who will see to your safety during the dreaming process as well as during your meditations and prayers.

Just as with angelic messages, you can most easily receive information from your spirit guides in the dream worlds. Tonight's technique will enhance your ability to perceive and understand the dream messages from your spirit guides.

Attuning Your Consciousness to the Guiding Angel

Gabriel, messenger of God, will be your guide tonight during your journey into the dream worlds. As the archangel most involved in helping you accomplish your life's mission, Gabriel is vitally interested in facilitating your connection to your spirit guides. He knows that their specialized knowledge can assist you in fulfilling your purpose for this lifetime. Before performing tonight's dream exercise, use the following invocation and contemplation to attune yourself to Gabriel's holy presence.

Invocation to Archangel Gabriel

> Gabriel, holy angel of God,
>   I ask you to come to me in my dreams tonight. Imbue me with the power of your strength as I commit to you my desire to create change in my life and to manifest my life's mission. In my dreams I make a place for our meeting. With courage I will meet you, and with courage I will take steps to bring into manifestation my mission in an effort to complete my soul's purpose and pattern for this lifetime. Amen.

Allow yourself to feel Gabriel's presence enter your heart. Next, to further attune your consciousness to the guiding presence for tonight, read and contemplate the following words.

> Purification of the self builds strength and opens the channels of communication between you and the beings on the higher planes. The wisdom of your guardian angel, the archangels, and your spirit guides is more easily understood and integrated by those who devote themselves to the purification of their heart and their mind.
>
> —ARCHANGEL GABRIEL

Allow these words to wash over you. Rest with them for a few minutes and feel your whole being come into alignment with their truth. Do this for a few minutes. You have now opened a conduit to the wisdom radiating from the author of tonight's contemplation—Archangel Gabriel. Open your eyes and continue tonight's session by performing the following dream exercise.

Tonight's Exercise: Meeting Your Spirit Guides

One of your spirit guides is waiting to meet with you in the dream worlds. To connect with your spirit guide you must first focus on the inner qualities or virtues that characterize the guide you wish to contact. For example, if you have a scientific problem you want help with, focus on the qualities of mind that a scientist would likely possess: dedication, drive, intellect, curiosity, problem-solving ability, and so on. Concentrate on these qualities for several minutes.

Next, offer a prayer of invocation to your chosen spirit guide. If you already know the name of your spirit guide, include it in the prayer, in the affirmation, and throughout the technique where appropriate.

> *Dear Spirit Guide,*
> *I ask that your messages be clear and your presence strong as I explore my dream worlds tonight. I trust in your guidance and accept your wisdom. I look forward to our meeting in my dreams. Amen.*

Focus on the specific type of help you need, and state your problem clearly by writing it down on a piece of paper or in your journal. You can clarify your problem by preparing some questions on the subject, writing them down as well. This will help your subconscious mind become versed in what your conscious mind would like an answer or solution to. It will also help your dream maker create a dream that reflects the wisdom message/solution being transmitted to you from your guide.

Finally, repeat an affirmation that reflects your desire to meet with the guide in the dream worlds to receive guidance and information. You can create your own affirmation or use the one provided. Remember to imbue your affirmation with strong, heartfelt desire. Repeat your affirmation several times.

> **Tonight in my dreams I will become aware of my spirit guide. I will clearly recognize and remember the lessons shared with me tonight.**

As you repeat this affirmation, feel the presence of your guide growing stronger and closer. Imagine that your own creative energies are reaching out, expanding, and merging with the creative essence of your guide. Continue to repeat the affirmation as you gently relax into a deep and restful sleep.

Don't worry if this technique doesn't produce immediate results. It takes time and practice to learn how to purify and open ourselves to these frequencies. Also, keep in mind that life on the other side of the veil is just as active and purposeful as this life. It is wise to remember that our friends in spirit may well be just as busy as we are, and it may take a few days before *they're* free to contact us.

Upon awakening in the morning, remember to lie still and keep your eyes closed. Focus your attention on accessing your dream memories. Take some time to allow your dream memories to impress themselves upon your waking mind. After a few minutes, record your dreams in your journal.

When you have finished, begin to unseal the messages hidden within your dreams. Call upon Archangel Gabriel to bring you insight as you interpret your dreams by saying the following prayer of invocation.

> *Dear Archangel Gabriel,*
>   *I ask that your messages be clear and your presence strong as I interpret my dreams today. I trust in your guidance and accept your divine help. I commit myself to the process of personal growth and the accomplishment of my personal mission. Amen.*

Next, perform all seven steps of the interpretation process. The seven steps (from chapter 3) are repeated for you below:

1. Make an inventory or list of each of the characters that appear in your dream, both human and nonhuman.

2. Examine your feelings about the dream characters.

3. Examine your role in the dream and your relationships to the dream characters.

4. Review the actions taking place in the dream.

5. Find out what aspect of yourself the dream characters represent by engaging them in imaginary conversation.

6. Analyze the dream setting (location/time of day/environment).

7. Consider your current life situation.

You will know that you have arrived at the correct dream interpretation when you feel something "click" within you. Don't be discouraged if this doesn't happen right away. The message of your dream may become unsealed over the course of the day or it may take even more time to emerge as you work through your spiritual growth issues.

Past-Life Dreaming

Dreaming of a past-life experience can have a healing affect upon our life. In past-life dreams we can often find answers to problems in the present as well as tap into talents that we have previously honed. Tonight's dream session examines how to access your past-life memories within the dream worlds. It also includes a past-life memory of Linda's as a sample of what you can expect to experience during past-life dreaming.

The experience of past-life dreaming is similar to the process one undergoes in a past-life regression. During a regression, an experienced facilitator leads the individual in the process of connecting to the wisdom and memories stored in the higher self. This same process can be used to access past-life memories in our dream worlds. Guided by the four archangels, your dream maker communicates with your higher self by injecting key memories from the past into your dream worlds. The main purpose of these memories is to uncover self-limiting patterns that affect your ability to function in your present life.

Exploration into past-life experiences should not be undertaken lightly or out of idle curiosity. These experiences are sacred, and we should treat them with the same respect we give our current life experiences. The main purpose of dreaming and dream exploration is to heal ourselves and our relationships so that we can grow and expand. Past-life exploration should also be approached in this manner. The goal is always to promote healing—usually emotional healing, but sometimes the healing of a physical pain that has its roots in a past traumatic experience.

Uncovering skills and abilities that we developed in earlier lifetimes can also create healing. Just as we can bring negative patterns with us, so too can we carry over positive patterns and abilities into our present lifetime. We can tap into these skill patterns and use them in our present life activities. It can be a tremendous boost to discover, for example, that we possess latent musical or artistic talent that was first developed in a past-life and that, with consistent effort, can again be brought forth in this lifetime.

Past-life recall and a past-life regression gave Linda insight into a lifetime where she had trained to serve as a leader and a visionary. It is interesting to note that Linda's focus for this regression was not to seek information about lifetimes as a seer or visionary. Her question for this particular regression was simply: "In what lifetime and under what circumstances did the pain in my lower back and spine originate?" The answer to this question took her to a lifetime in Ancient Egypt.

As you will see, the regression not only answered Linda's question but it also provided her with new information and insights into a prior life's mission, patterns, and latent abilities. While this example was from a waking past-life regression, the principles and learning power of accessing past-life memories in the dream worlds is just as potent.

Linda's Egyptian Experience

This life experience feels as if it was as least 2000 years before Christ—perhaps even earlier. I was a male in this lifetime, dressed in an expensive tunic of soft white linen. As a young prince of Egypt, not yet eighteen years old, I was rigorously groomed and prepared for an important leadership role in the service of my people (excavations have shown that thousands of mini-princes and minor pharaohs lived in ancient Egypt).

The Egyptian priests had responsibility for a large amount of my training, and under their instruction I learned important spiritual disciplines. Part of my daily routine included rising early in the morning before daybreak. I then walked to a pyramid and climbed to the top of it (I feel it was one of the pyramids at Giza—for the word Giza was strongly impressed upon me during my regression and subsequently during a past-life recall exercise). Having reached the summit of the pyramid, I sat down and crossed my legs (somewhat similar to a lotus position), closed my eyes, cleared my mind, and meditated in the manner that the priests had taught me.

This meditation method involved bringing the energy and life-force of the sun into my body and chakra system. I would literally "drink in" the warmth and power of the sun down through the top of my head, into my neck and spine, and finally throughout my whole body/chakra system. When fully illumined by the light of the sun (it seemed to take at least an hour or two to reach this point), I would then be ready to receive the visions that would help me lead my people.

These daily meditations were an important part of my spiritual training and self-discipline as a young prince-in-training. Unfortunately, in this lifetime I did not live long enough to take over the leadership role I had been so carefully groomed for. I was killed in my very first battle by some type of spear being driven through my lower spine. The next scene of my regression brought me to the life review process that one undergoes after death. In this life review I connected with the feelings of my former personality—the young Egyptian prince.

The feelings of the prince that I tapped into included a deep sense of failure and grief over not having had the opportunity to complete his life mission—for the young prince had been killed before he had a chance to fulfill his role as leader and guardian of his people. He felt bad that he had let his people down by being killed in his first battle, and he worried over their fate because he could not be there to guide them with the visionary ability he had so rigorously honed.

What did Linda learn from this regression? She learned the probable origin of her lower back pain as well as important information about her former meditation practices and disciplines. She saw how the skills and disciplines acquired in that former lifetime (which were not given a chance to mature) could now be tapped into and used to promote personal growth in this lifetime.

Attuning Your Consciousness to the Guiding Angel

Michael, chief of the archangels, will be your guide tonight during your journey into the dream worlds. Before performing tonight's dream exercise, use the following invocation and contemplation to attune yourself to his holy presence.

Invocation to Archangel Michael

Michael, holy angel of God,
*   I invite you into my dream worlds and into my consciousness. I seek to uncover and understand the truth of my choices and to accept the results of all that I have put into action. Please help me to see myself more clearly and lend me the wisdom of your words and presence as I move to lift the Chalice of Justice and wield the Sword of Truth. Amen.*

Allow yourself to feel Michael's presence enter your heart. Next, to further attune your consciousness to the guiding presence for tonight, read and contemplate the following words.

> Understanding soul's purpose lies in understanding soul's pattern. Everything is as it should be at this moment of time, including the fact that you are now deciding to become a conscious integrated being on all levels.
>
> —Archangel Michael

Allow these words to wash over you. Rest with them for a few minutes and feel your whole being come into alignment with their truth. Do this for a few minutes. You have now opened a conduit to the wisdom radiating from the author of tonight's contemplation—Archangel Michael. Open your eyes and continue tonight's session by performing the following dream exercise.

Tonight's Exercise: Past-Life Dreaming

Your past includes past lifetimes—your consciousness before this present incarnation. Tonight you will dream of a past life that is important for you to consider in regard to your present life circumstances. Every choice you have made has had an impact in bringing you to this present moment. We are all linked to the infinite past.

As you go to sleep tonight say the following prayer several times. It will help set the tone for your night's dreams.

> *Dear Archangel Michael,*
> *Please show me past-life memories during my dreams. Help me to see my past in a clear light. I desire to learn how my past is affecting my present. I ask this of you through the universal Christ energy. Amen.*

As you repeat this prayer, feel the presence of Archangel Michael growing stronger and closer. Continue to repeat the prayer and gently relax into a deep and restful sleep knowing that soon Michael will unseal past-life memories for you to view. He will be there to protect and shield you from any memories that are too painful to view in the present.

Upon awakening in the morning, remember to lie still and keep your eyes closed. Focus your attention on accessing your dream memories. Take some time to allow your dream memories to impress themselves upon your waking mind. After a few minutes, record your dreams in your journal.

When you have finished, begin to unseal the messages hidden within your dreams. Call upon Archangel Michael to bring you insight as you interpret your dreams by saying the following prayer of invocation.

> *Dear Archangel Michael,*
> *Please shine your light of truth upon my dream messages.*
> *Help me to unseal their wisdom so that I might better under-*
> *stand myself, my relationships, and my mission for this lifetime.*
> *Amen.*

Next, perform all seven steps of the interpretation process. The seven steps (from chapter 3) are repeated for you below:

1. Make an inventory or list of each of the characters that appear in your dream, both human and nonhuman.
2. Examine your feelings about the dream characters.
3. Examine your role in the dream and your relationships to the dream characters.
4. Review the actions taking place in the dream.
5. Find out what aspect of yourself the dream characters represent by engaging them in imaginary conversation.
6. Analyze the dream setting (location/time of day/environment).
7. Consider your current life situation.

You will know that you have arrived at the correct dream interpretation when you feel something "click" within you. Don't be discouraged if this doesn't happen right away. The message of your dream may become unsealed over the course of the day or it may take even more time to emerge as you work through your spiritual growth issues.

Creative Dreaming

Creative dreaming is the process of solving your daily problems within the dream worlds. Your problem can be as simple as a work-related issue, or more complex, as in the direction to take in a personal relationship, or even the solution to an intellectual pursuit.

Creative dreaming, also known as problem-solving dreams, has been used for centuries by inventors, philosophers, and rulers. Thomas Edison, for instance, reportedly received solutions to his waking-world problems in the dream state. This remarkable ability is not restricted to the great scientists of the past, for we have each been endowed with the faculty of imagination. Tonight you'll learn how to use the dream worlds to find solutions to the important problems in your life.

One of the most helpful dreams we can have is a problem-solving dream. During our nightly sleep we can access information from other realms of existence. These other realms include our own wisdom pool, which is stored in our higher self. We can also access information from other personalities we may encounter in the dream state as well as from higher energies emanating from the angelic and spiritual realms.

During creative dreams the dream self employs our imagination to run through thousands of possibilities regarding a current problem or creative question we may have. These possibilities are considered in other realities outside the current dream environment. You will not be aware (either consciously or from a dream viewpoint) that a part of your self is processing multiple solutions to your problem or question. Once an answer has been sufficiently formulated by your "inner processor," it is injected into the dream environment, thus showing itself within your dreams.

The problem-solving/creative dream can take literal or symbolic form. Therefore good dream interpretation skills greatly enhance your understanding of problem-solving dreams. Often a solution will seem clear when you are in the dream but may not make sense when you awaken. If you have this experience, write down as many details as you can remember about your dream.

Often reviewing the details of the dream in this way will restore an understanding of how the answer you received can be logically applied in your waking world.

One of the most important aspects of creative dreaming is learning to pose your question to your dream maker in a way that returns the desired result. For example, if you have a problem speaking in front of large groups of people and you wish to receive guidance from your dream maker, you should *not* ask: "Why am I such a goof when I talk in front of people—what is wrong with me?" Rather, you will obtain better results by rephrasing your question: "How can I learn to effectively communicate my true message to people, especially when I am nervous and unsure of what to say?"

A few years ago Peter learned an important lesson in a dream. He was confused about his employment status and did not know whether he should switch jobs. The decision weighed heavily on his mind for several days. Unsure of the direction to take, he looked to his dream worlds for an answer. Then he dreamed that he had indeed changed jobs. During the dream he had the experience of working for a new employer.

He quickly realized that he was not happy with this new position. He fervently wished that he had not quit his previous job. This dream was so powerful to Peter that it felt like an actual, physical experience. When he awoke the next morning he was relieved to find that he had only been dreaming. He promptly took the advice of his dream and chose to stay at his current job. In this way, Peter avoided making a decision in his waking world that he could not undo as easily as in the dream worlds.

Attuning Your Consciousness to the Guiding Angel

Gabriel, messenger of God, will be your guide tonight during your journey into the dream worlds. Before performing tonight's dream exercise, use the following invocation and contemplation to attune yourself to his holy presence.

Invocation to Archangel Gabriel

Gabriel, holy angel of God,
I ask you to come to me in my dreams tonight. Imbue me with the power of your strength as I commit to you my desire to create change in my life and to manifest my life's mission. In my dreams I make a place for our meeting. With courage I will meet you, and with courage I will take steps to bring into manifestation my mission in an effort to complete my soul's purpose and pattern for this lifetime. Amen.

Allow yourself to feel Gabriel's presence enter your heart. Next, to further attune your consciousness to the guiding presence for tonight, read and contemplate the following words.

> The One Energy of God is, has always been, and shall always be. The world is without end, for the energy that creates the world shall never dissipate nor vanish.
>
> —ARCHANGEL GABRIEL

Allow these words to wash over you. Rest with them for a few minutes and feel your whole being come into alignment with their truth. Do this for a few minutes. You have now opened a conduit to the wisdom radiating from the author of tonight's contemplation—Archangel Gabriel. Open your eyes and continue tonight's session by performing the following dream exercise.

Tonight's Exercise: Inducing a Problem-Solving Dream

Problem-solving dreams happen to be one of the few types of dreams that are very susceptible to your personal induction. The main factor in inducing a problem-solving dream is to query your inner self directly before bed. As Christ said, "Ask, and Ye Shall Receive," so too can you ask your wisdom self any question that you desire. It will then find, formulate, and present an answer to you in your dreams. Here are the steps to induce a problem-solving dream.

1. Prepare for bed in your usual manner.
2. As your body relaxes keep your attention focused on the screen of your mind. Imagine a white screen, as in a theater.
3. Formulate your question; make it clear and address it to your wisdom self. State it in such a way as to elicit a positive response (i.e., "How can I _____" rather than "Why can't I _____").
4. See your question appear on the blank screen of your mind.
5. As you fall asleep know that you have sent your question to your creative subconscious and that your dream worlds will present a solution to you.

You should awaken with a dream world memory that contains the solution (or a seed to the solution) to your problem. Sometimes, you will not remember having a dream at all. Yet the answer to the problem will come to your conscious awareness later in the day.

Upon awakening in the morning, remember to lie still and keep your eyes closed. Focus your attention on accessing your dream memories. Take some time to allow your dream memories to impress themselves upon your waking mind. After a few minutes, record your dreams in your journal.

When you have finished, begin to unseal the messages hidden within your dreams. Call upon Archangel Gabriel to bring you insight as you interpret your dreams by saying the following prayer of invocation.

> *Dear Archangel Gabriel,*
>   *I ask that your messages be clear and your presence strong as I interpret my dreams today. I trust in your guidance and accept your divine help. I commit myself to the process of personal growth and the accomplishment of my personal mission. Amen.*

Next, perform all seven steps of the interpretation process. The seven steps (from chapter 3) are repeated for you below:

1. Make an inventory or list of each of the characters that appear in your dream, both human and nonhuman.

2. Examine your feelings about the dream characters.

3. Examine your role in the dream and your relationships to the dream characters.

4. Review the actions taking place in the dream.

5. Find out what aspect of yourself the dream characters represent by engaging them in imaginary conversation.

6. Analyze the dream setting (location/time of day/environment).

7. Consider your current life situation.

You will know that you have arrived at the correct dream interpretation when you feel something "click" within you. Don't be discouraged if this doesn't happen right away. The message of your dream may become unsealed over the course of the day or it may take even more time to emerge as you work through your spiritual growth issues.

Prophetic Dreams

Prophetic dreams offer you the chance to dream of future events. Prophetic dreams warn you of situations that require you to modify your actions in order to avoid problems or to take advantage of unseen opportunities. Tonight we'll explore this subject and provide you with an exercise that can influence your dream maker to create prophetic dreams.

Prophetic dreams foretell some aspect of the future. For example, whenever Linda's mother dreamed of picking berries, especially blueberries or strawberries, someone in her extended family got sick or died within a few days. Linda's mother did not fear this dream; rather, she appreciated the warning it provided her. It reminded her not to take the presence of her relatives for granted.

A second example of this type of dream comes from an acquaintance of Linda's who often has prophetic dreams. This woman's most recent prophetic dreams focused on her sister. In each dream, she saw her sister covered in blood. Shortly after having these dreams, she discovered that her sister had undergone surgery to control an unexpected bleeding problem.

Prophetic dreams can both warn and give us advice. Peter had a prophetic dream that also served as an advisory dream. Even though he knew that he should follow his dream's advice, his conscious mind found reasons (excuses) not to. He still regrets that decision. The following is Peter's account of this prophetic dream.

> During my early years I had many difficult experiences that I failed to effectively process. This led me to make choices based on fear rather than self-knowledge. I experienced my mother's death to ovarian cancer; joined a cult; got married and had kids; and chose to ignore my father. I refused to have any form of relationship with him. I came to believe (in my youthful ignorance) that I knew more then he did. The cult I had joined did little to dissuade that viewpoint. In fact, the leaders of the cult

often referred to those outside the group as enemies of the master. They also downplayed and devalued the role of one's mother, father, and family.

Even before I became involved with the cult, my relationship with my father was not ideal. It was primarily one of fear and obedience. He was a loud man with a volatile temper, who often argued with my mother. I learned to fear and respect his temper at a very young age. Because of this I did not know how to relate to him in any other way. After my mother's death (when I was sixteen), I withdrew from him even more.

It wasn't until three months before my prophetic dream (at age thirty-eight) that I finally connected with my father. I had not spoken with him for more than eight years. When I finally did call him (during my divorce process) I learned he had also gone through a difficult divorce from his second wife after a marriage of twenty years.

During this conversation I discovered that my father had changed. He talked to me differently. In fact, he had never talked to me in such a positive, direct, and revealing manner before. The experiences of life had finally brought out his loving side. I found this unexpected change very positive. It signaled a new opportunity in our relationship.

My father lived in Seattle at the time of the dream. After talking with him on the telephone a few times, I decided that I wanted to visit him. I too had been changed by life. I was moving out of a failed marriage and slowly extricating myself from a journey of eighteen years within a very disempowering cult. There was so much I wanted to share with my father— face to face. I had so much to say, feel, and learn. Due to financial constraints, I decided to wait a few months before Linda and I could fly out to visit with my father. Shortly after making the decision to postpone my trip I had the following dream.

THE STOPPED CLOCK

I was in a room with my father. It was night and the lights were on in the room. I recall seeing a wall clock. The clock's shape was that of the sun. Extending from the clock were twelve long tapered spokes that made the clock resemble a shining star. As I looked at the clock, I realized that it had stopped. Its arms did not move. Then I became aware that the electricity to the room had been cut off and that was why the wall clock did not function.

I awoke from the dream. As I thought about its meaning, a part of me knew it held an important message. But instead of taking the time to figure out its meaning (and hidden warning), I ignored the voice of my inner conscience. Then, only three months later, my father died of a sudden heart attack at age sixty-nine. I never had the opportunity to visit him, learn from him, or share with him all that I had wanted to share. The meaning and purpose of my dream became much clearer to me then—although my realization came much too late.

The clock represented time. The electricity symbolized the energy that powers the heart. The lack of electricity and the stopped clock pointed out that time was running short and that the energy that powered my father's heart would suddenly stop. The electric lights being on (in spite of the power outage) was a strong signal for me to realize that I was aware (at some level) of my father's impending health crisis.

Part of my inner self knew the dream was important, but I did not follow its guidance. I did not take the time to properly analyze its message and take appropriate action. Now I am left to regret the missed opportunities. I have since committed to heeding the messages of my dreams, no matter how tired I am or how easy it may be to say, "It was just a dream."

Attuning Your Consciousness to the Guiding Angel

Michael, chief of the archangels, will be your guide tonight during your journey into the dream worlds. Before performing tonight's dream exercise, use the following invocation and contemplation to attune yourself to his holy presence.

Invocation to Archangel Michael

Michael, holy angel of God,
   I invite you into my dream worlds and into my consciousness. I seek to uncover and understand the truth of my choices and to accept the results of all that I have put into action. Please help me to see myself more clearly and lend me the wisdom of your words and presence as I move to lift the Chalice of Justice and wield the Sword of Truth. Amen.

Allow yourself to feel Michael's presence enter your heart. Next, to further attune your consciousness to the guiding presence for tonight, read and contemplate the following words.

> Experience is why the soul chose to spin the embodiments that you are now conscious of. This experience is for the benefit of the integrated self. It is a gift from God.
>
> —ARCHANGEL MICHAEL

Allow these words to wash over you. Rest with them for a few minutes and feel your whole being come into alignment with their truth. Do this for a few minutes. You have now opened a conduit to the wisdom radiating from the author of tonight's contemplation—Archangel Michael. Open your eyes and continue tonight's session by performing the following dream exercise.

Tonight's Exercise: Dreaming the Future

Time and space are the elements in which we define our experience in the earth worlds. Some people believe time to be linear (one moment following the next); others believe multiple concurrent layers of time can coexist. In any case, what we experience is a result of choices—the rearranging and interaction of energy patterns. The future is therefore foreseeable. Our degree of accuracy in seeing the future lies in our ability to perceive the energy patterns of all beings and elements of nature, and the Creator.

We can see the future in our dreams, for in the dream worlds we have access to information beyond our conscious awareness. We can then synthesize probable future events (including what we can do to change that future). To prepare for your dreams tonight, say the following prayer to Michael several times.

> Dear Michael,
>   Please show me my future and how my choices will create that future. I desire to know this so I can change my present in order to bring greater peace, understanding, and love into the world. This I ask of you through the universal Christ energy. Amen.

As you repeat this prayer, feel the presence of Archangel Michael growing stronger and closer. Continue to repeat the prayer and gently relax into a deep and restful sleep, knowing that soon Michael will show you a glimpse into your future, either in literal or symbolic images, during your dreams.

Upon awakening in the morning, remember to lie still and keep your eyes closed. Focus your attention on accessing your dream memories. Take some time to allow your dream memories to impress themselves upon your waking mind. After a few minutes, record your dreams in your journal.

When you have finished, begin to unseal the messages hidden within your dreams. Call upon Archangel Michael to bring you insight as you interpret your dreams by saying the following prayer of invocation.

> *Dear Archangel Michael,*
> *Please shine your light of truth upon my dream messages.*
> *Help me to unseal their wisdom so that I might better under-*
> *stand myself, my relationships, and my mission for this lifetime.*
> *Amen.*

Next, perform all seven steps of the interpretation process. The seven steps (from chapter 3) are repeated for you below:

1. Make an inventory or list of each of the characters that appear in your dream, both human and nonhuman.
2. Examine your feelings about the dream characters.
3. Examine your role in the dream and your relationships to the dream characters.
4. Review the actions taking place in the dream.
5. Find out what aspect of yourself the dream characters represent by engaging them in imaginary conversation.
6. Analyze the dream setting (location/time of day/environment).
7. Consider your current life situation.

You will know that you have arrived at the correct dream interpretation when you feel something "click" within you. Don't be discouraged if this doesn't happen right away. The message of your dream may become unsealed over the course of the day or it may take even more time to emerge as you work through your spiritual growth issues.

Contacting Your Deceased Loved Ones

Tonight you will learn how you can contact your deceased loved ones in the dream worlds. You will also be shown the difference between a dream in which the characters represent a part of your personality and one in which there is actual spiritual contact with your deceased loved ones in the dream worlds.

Most of us have experienced the pain and sadness of not being able to express our feelings of love and caring to those loved ones who have passed away. We long to speak to them and share with them the tenderness we hold for them deep within our hearts. But the opportunity for that has passed away, along with our loved one. Or has it?

We believe that it is possible to contact our deceased loved ones in the dream worlds. How do we know this is possible? Because we have experienced it. While we cannot prove the truth of this contact, we can share with you our personal experience of it. And, more importantly, we can explain how to tell the difference between a dream in which the characters represent a part of your personality and one in which you have actual spiritual contact with deceased loved ones.

Telling the Difference

The purpose of dreams in which the characters represent parts of yourself is to heal and integrate the unheard and repressed parts of your personality. In such dreams, you feel a lack of connection to your deceased loved ones. Your loved ones behave in uncharacteristic ways that seem to lack clarity and purpose.

You can tell that the characters in your dreams are not your actual loved ones when your interactions with them simply don't make sense to your conscious mind. Neither of you treat each other as you normally would have in waking life, when your loved one was still alive. Indeed, in these dreams you actually feel *disconnected* from your loved ones because you can't understand why they are behaving in the manner they are, nor can you understand why you are behaving strangely toward them.

In other words, the behavior and the feelings invoked by the characters within this type of dream do not match with what your conscious, waking mind knows to be true. This is because your dream maker is trying to make you aware of some hidden and hurting part of yourself that you have lost touch with or perhaps never even knew existed. Your dream maker uses the characteristics of your deceased loved ones to make you aware of traits that you possess. It creates a drama in which these characteristics become apparent to you. They may be characteristics that you don't like, or feelings and tendencies within you that you deny ownership of in the waking world.

In order to become whole, we must acknowledge, listen to, and then fully integrate these lost or hidden parts of our personality. Otherwise we will keep spinning around in circles within our own self-made and self-limiting patterns. We hold these self-limiting patterns together through our fear of who we are, of who we have been, and even of the beauty of all we know we can become.

In contrast, a dream in which you actually visit with the spirit of deceased loved ones is marked by its vibrancy and purpose. Your loved ones usually appear glowing with health, looking years younger than when they passed away. And they usually have a message for you that lets you know they still exist and are doing fine in their new world. Sometimes they express their worry about those they left behind. They may send you a message like the one Peter received several months after his father passed away. In Peter's dream his father appeared and said in a very direct and clear manner, "Take care of your brother. He needs you now."

Linda has had several dreams in which she conversed with the dead. She recently had a series of dreams of her deceased mother. These particular dreams (included below) are good examples of the information you can elicit about the conditions in the afterlife. Do not be surprised if the information you elicit from your deceased relatives/friends differs from one person to the next, and from one dream to the next. Remember, your loved ones are still learning and acquiring information about their new environment. In addition, each one of us, living or dead, experiences reality differently.

We each have our own lens through which we interpret the world. The way two people describe the same event (or even the same photograph, for example) can vary remarkably, depending upon their attitudes, beliefs, and the way they tend to view life. It is no different for the dead. They are essentially the same people they were before they died. While their viewpoint has expanded somewhat because they no longer have the density of a physical body, they still have the personality they had while in physical life. This continues to influence their perceptions and attitudes.

Linda will now share the series of dreams that she had of her mother (these dreams came about three months after her mother passed away).

I'M STILL HERE

I was sitting in a room filled with family members. Suddenly I noticed Mom appear among them. No one else had noticed her appearance—but I exclaimed: "Mom, it's you! You're here and you've finally come to visit!" "Yes," she answered. She looked very intense but seemed glad that I could see her. I could touch/hug her too, and I did. She was still thin (as she was in the hospital), but she seemed much healthier and more vibrant than before she died. She wore a blue outfit. I told her we all missed her and had been hoping to reach her in the dream worlds. As we talked, her presence became more substantial.

Linda then woke up briefly, feeling happy to have had this dream. She then fell back to sleep and continued to dream of her mother.

I'M STILL HERE, PART 2

I was sitting at a table when Mom appeared again. I was so happy to see her materialize. This time she appeared even more vibrant. She wore shades of light and dark blue. Her hair was dark brown—no gray at all. I then asked her several questions: "Did you see any relatives/friends when you first passed away (were any relatives there to greet you when you died)?" She answered, "Yes, I saw the Cronins (family friends) and also some others."

Then my deceased uncle Leo suddenly materialized at the table, as if to reassure me that he was with her.

As a side note, you might be interested in knowing that when my mother was on her deathbed I had asked her if she could see any relatives or angels waiting on the other side for her, and she answered "yes,"—she saw both relatives and angels there. I asked her if she could see Uncle Leo and Grandma, and she replied, "Yes, they are both there." We had discussed what happens after death many times, and in fact she had told me that her own father had experienced visions of angels shortly before his death in 1947.

I asked Mom if she was okay. She replied that she was fine, but there was an intensity about her as well as a feeling of sorrow.

When I asked her about the dying process she started to disappear. She was still there, but somehow less present. Suddenly another relative appeared: my Aunt Dorothy. She had passed away several years before Mom. Dorothy appeared more healthy and vibrant than I'd ever seen her look during her life. She explained to me that death doesn't bring an instant resolution of problems—we still have to deal with our self-judgment, and that was what Mom was working on. I felt then that Mom must not be in heaven yet. But I couldn't know for sure so I asked my mom, "Are you in heaven?" She did not answer right away. Instead she said she had to leave to attend a prayer vigil training. As she was leaving, she answered my question by saying, "No, I am not in heaven yet." I then asked her if she was in purgatory (Mom was Roman Catholic), and she answered, "Yes." Then I asked her if there was a hell. She answered, "Yes," and indicated that this was part of the purpose of the prayer vigil—to pray for the people in hell.

It is interesting to note that Linda's mother seemed to know more about her afterlife environment each time Linda dreamed of her. Linda saw a definite progression in her mother's knowledge as well as her apparent state of happiness. Linda will now share with you another dream she had of her mother several months later.

YOUTHFUL MOM

This was a very lucid dream of Mom. We were sitting in a room by the north window. I was so happy to see her again; I said, "Mom, you're here!" Then I said, "But you're not really here in a living body, are you?" She answered, "No, I'm not." But I could still give her a hug, and it felt so good. I said to her, "Mom, I'm sorry I didn't always show you how much I cared about you." She said, "That's okay," as peace radiated from her. Her face was relaxed and tranquil. That is when I "woke up" within my dream. I knew I was lucid dreaming and that I could consciously ask her anything I wanted. She was sharply dressed in a very nice suit/skirt combination and looked very trim and young (she seemed about thirty-five or forty years old, which is half the age she was when she died). Her long hair flowed (curled) as it did in pictures of her when she was quite young. She seemed very beautiful and peaceful, yet I could still tell she didn't seem 100 percent happy. Again I asked her several questions about the afterlife. Here

is the one I remember: "Mom, can you see and hear God?" She
answered, "No, but I do have more of an awareness of Him and
His love." In this dream she tried to communicate to me that death
is a continuation of life—of the same state of awareness you have
while in the body—and yet it is somewhat expanded. I marveled
at how good she looked, and I told her that I loved her and missed
her. She said she understood. Her aura was one of quiet peace.

While Linda has related her dream communication as if it were a conversation, it was more like a mind-to-mind or telepathic experience. This type of dream communication is another characteristic of what we believe to be actual spiritual encounters with other beings during the dream state. When trying to decide on the validity of your experience, keep in mind the characteristics of a visitation dream, summarized here for your reference.

Visitation Dreams

- Visitation dreams are unusually vivid.
- Your loved ones, if elderly at the time of their death, appear vibrantly healthy and often years younger. Deceased children will often appear to have gotten older, just as they would have if they had lived on in the physical world.
- The deceased have a loving, positive message that they strongly desire to convey to you.
- You are lucid and aware (in the dream) that those you are communicating with are actually dead.
- The deceased loved ones are usually aware that they are dead and often answer your questions about the afterlife.
- You are aware the visitants are dead, yet you accept that they are still alive in a spiritual body. Their spiritual body has substance. You can feel their reality within the dream state by touching and hugging them.
- You seem to communicate with them more by mind telepathy than by verbal conversation.
- The deceased interact with you in a manner consistent with how they did when alive.

Attuning Your Consciousness to the Guiding Angel

Raphael, archangel of healing, wholeness, and acceptance, will be your guide tonight during your journey into the dream worlds. Before performing tonight's dream exercise, use the following invocation and contemplation to attune yourself to his holy presence.

Invocation to Archangel Raphael

> *Raphael, holy angel of God,*
> *I desire to know your healing presence. I have made a place*
> *in my heart for your visitation. Come to me in my dreams*
> *tonight and share with me your wisdom and love as I move to*
> *express my innermost thoughts and feelings. I desire to know*
> *God and to love myself again. Raphael, help me to express and*
> *then heal my pain. I await you in hopeful anticipation of your*
> *radiant presence. Amen.*

Allow yourself to feel Raphael's presence enter your heart. Next, to further attune your consciousness to the guiding presence for tonight, read and contemplate the following words.

> When change comes, it is like the breath of the wind in the
> sails of a ship that has been adrift on the seas. Learn to navigate
> through the worlds by adjusting the sail of your discernment.
>
> —ARCHANGEL RAPHAEL

Allow these words to wash over you. Rest with them for a few minutes and feel your whole being come into alignment with their truth. Do this for a few minutes. You have now opened a conduit to the wisdom radiating from the author of tonight's contemplation—Archangel Raphael. Open your eyes and continue tonight's session by performing the following dream exercise.

Tonight's Exercise: Contacting Your Deceased Loved Ones in the Dream Worlds

Do you ever wish you could visit a friend or loved one who has passed on to the other side? You can in your dream worlds! The dream worlds serve as a bridge between the physical and the invisible worlds.

Upon retiring, relax and then choose one relative or loved one that has passed on. Imagine this loved one is standing in front of you, and say the following affirmation.

> I *will* speak with _____ (state person's name)
> in my dreams tonight.

Imagine what you would like to say to your loved one. Think about his or her unique personal qualities and about how much you still care about this person. Then repeat the affirmation several more times as you fall asleep. Relax as you move into the dream worlds, knowing that Archangel Raphael will guide you to your loved one.

———————

Upon awakening in the morning, remember to lie still and keep your eyes closed. Focus your attention on accessing your dream memories. Take some time to allow your dream memories to impress themselves upon your waking mind. After a few minutes, record your dreams in your journal.

When you have finished, begin to unseal the messages hidden within your dreams. Call upon Archangel Raphael to bring you insight as you interpret your dreams by saying the following prayer of invocation.

> *Dear Archangel Raphael,*
>   *Send your healing light to illuminate my consciousness that I might better understand the dream messages imparted by the spirits of my loved ones. Amen.*

Next, perform all seven steps of the interpretation process. The seven steps (from chapter 3) are repeated for you below:

1. Make an inventory or list of each of the characters that appear in your dream, both human and nonhuman.
2. Examine your feelings about the dream characters.
3. Examine your role in the dream and your relationships to the dream characters.
4. Review the actions taking place in the dream.
5. Find out what aspect of yourself the dream characters represent by engaging them in imaginary conversation.
6. Analyze the dream setting (location/time of day/environment).
7. Consider your current life situation.

You will know that you have arrived at the correct dream interpretation when you feel something "click" within you. Don't be discouraged if this doesn't happen right away. The message of your dream may become unsealed over the course of the day or it may take even more time to emerge as you work through your spiritual growth issues.

Dreaming for Others

Tonight you will learn how to help others by incubating a dream specifically for them. Dreaming for others is an especially helpful technique that one can use to assist people who cannot yet recall any of their own dreams. You will use both your dream world navigation skills and your dream interpretation skills to access information for others.

You have already learned that the dream worlds give voice to the concerns of our subconscious and of the different parts of the self. Our soul self speaks to us in dreams, as does our higher self and our emotional self. When we dream of water, for example, it is usually the emotional self letting us know we need to acknowledge and express certain feelings. At times, even God and the angels speak to us in our dreams, giving us insight and direction.

But can we dream for others? Can we learn to navigate the dream worlds, searching for information that exists in other realities, beyond the operating level of our conscious mind? Yes! Just as we typically only tap into a small fraction of our brain power on a given day, we typically use only a small portion of our abilities to traverse the dream worlds.

The Power of Imagination and Belief

Our belief in something gives it the power to become reality. Likewise, our belief in our own ability to accomplish a goal gives us the power to achieve it. Our beliefs can either limit us or empower us! Consider the following: We are limited only by our ability to imagine and by our will to believe. If history's greatest minds had not dared to imagine and believe in possibilities, then most of the twentieth century's greatest achievements simply would not exist. Think of it: If Leonardo Da Vinci and the Wright brothers had not dreamed of and believed in the possibility of flight, would we now have the ability to traverse the earth and space itself with the speed and ease we take for granted?

Just as these visionaries looked beyond a belief system that might have limited their achievements, we can conceive of realities that exist beyond the perception of our five senses. "Whatever the mind can conceive, it can and will achieve," is as true for our dream world exploration as it is for our waking physical reality.

Navigating the Dream Worlds

Learning to navigate the dream worlds requires three things: belief, desire, and commitment. Your belief system can either help or hinder your ability to have the dream experiences you desire. For example, Linda's mother placed a high value on dream study and strongly encouraged her children to remember and interpret their dreams. This helped Linda to adopt a belief system within which her dreamscapes had validity and importance. She developed an understanding of her personal dream symbols as she learned to traverse the different layers of reality within the dream worlds.

Thus, if you want to navigate and explore the dream worlds, you must first *believe* that it is possible. Second, you need to generate the desire to accomplish it. And third, you need to make an ongoing commitment to explore, chart, and expand your dream world experiences.

Your commitment gains strength when you consistently take the time to remember and record your dreams. Over time this will help you to create a literal map of your dream worlds. The information in chapter 3, "Dreamwork Basics," will help you to create this map.

In the process of charting your dream worlds you will develop important dream interpretation skills that will help you to understand your dream experiences. You will discern the meaning of your personal dream symbols and with practice you will learn which part of yourself each dream character represents.

In addition, you will know when your dream characters represent a visitation with beings from the higher realms and when they represent a part of you. The more you study your dreams, the more clear they will become. As a result, your faith in your ability to correctly decipher the source and meaning of your dream messages will grow. Empowered by your success, you can help others interpret their dreams, and perhaps one day you may even choose to dream for them.

The Dream Oracle

What is it like to travel the dream worlds? This depends on your reason for your journey. For example, you might wish to contact a deceased relative or an angelic being. Or you might search for specific information regarding a waking-world problem or situation, as Linda did in a former lifetime when she served as a dream oracle. To give you an example of this, Linda will share the story of when she served as a dream oracle in ancient Persia.

Linda's Story—the Dream Oracle

Knowledge of my lifetime as a dream oracle in ancient Persia came to me in three ways: past-life dreams, several readings with psychic counselors, and past-life recall memories that arose while I journaled. The personal readings were done eighteen years apart, with two different psychics, who both tapped into this Persian lifetime. In the readings, the psychics brought out similar information. The essence of my Persian dream oracle experience is as follows.

> I was a young woman with dark skin and hair, veiled and dressed in flowing robes. I lived with my sister priestesses in a temple dedicated to wisdom gathering. I was the one known to have "the Word." During a session with me (the dream oracle), people would present their questions and concerns. Then, later that night I would have a dream for them that contained "the Word," which held the answer to their questions and concerns.
>
> Knowledge of my abilities spread throughout Persia. I was successful in helping many people over a period of ten years. At the end of this ten-year period a large family came to me for advice. They needed to know whether they would have safe passage on a long journey they had planned; at that time the warring tribes in the land could make travel very dangerous. That night I had a dream for them, and, based on this dream, I assured them that they would have safe passage.
>
> As it turned out, the whole family was massacred on their journey. When I learned of their fate I felt devastated. Heartbroken and filled with guilt, I withdrew from the world. My fellow sister priestesses pleaded with me to return to the temple and to continue serving as the oracle. But I refused to ever dream for anyone again, for my gift had failed me. I felt I could no longer trust it. I lived out the rest of that lifetime as a hermit.

The psychics who gave me this reading told me not to feel bad about this failure, for even the best psychics in the world are correct only about 80 percent of the time. Despite their reassurances, I feel that I am still affected by the emotional residue from that Persian lifetime. Because of the strong emotional patterns from that lifetime, I spent many subsequent lives in isolation. Regressions have revealed lifetimes spent as a cloistered nun in Mexico, in Spain, and in Germany as well as lifetimes lived as a hermit—denying myself the relationships of spouse, friends, and family.

Dreaming for Others

After reading of Linda's traumatic experience as a dream oracle in Persia, you may wonder why anyone would want to dream for others. The answer is simply this: to share your gifts. Yes, people do make mistakes, and sometimes we do misinterpret our dreams. Sometimes our mistakes can hurt others. But imagine what would happen if no one took the risk to help others.

What if heart surgeons were so afraid of making mistakes that they refused to operate? What would happen if airline pilots refused to fly for fear of making a mistake that might cause the death of their passengers? Obviously the world would come to a near standstill if we were all afraid to risk helping others.

Each day we face a multitude of choices. We can choose to be loving and helpful, courageous and life-promoting. Or we can choose to shut down, isolate ourselves, and withhold all that we are from the world, just as Linda did in the latter part of her Persian lifetime and in several lifetimes that followed. What choice will you make today?

Attuning Your Consciousness to the Guiding Angel

Michael, chief of the archangels, will be your guide tonight during your journey into the dream worlds. Before performing tonight's dream exercise, use the following invocation and contemplation to attune yourself to his holy presence.

Invocation to Archangel Michael

> *Michael, holy angel of God,*
> *I invite you into my dream worlds and into my consciousness.*
> *I seek to understand the workings of cause and effect and the*
> *interconnectedness of human life. Please help me to see myself*
> *and others more clearly as I navigate within the dream worlds.*
> *Lend me the wisdom of your words and presence as I move to lift*
> *the Chalice of Justice and wield the Sword of Truth. Amen.*

Allow yourself to feel Michael's presence enter your heart. Next, to further attune your consciousness to the guiding presence for tonight, read and contemplate the following words.

> Meditate upon your gifts. Hold them lovingly in your
> heart and they will flower within you, just as a seed grows
> when exposed to the warmth of the sun. Share what you have
> learned with others, for it is the sharing process itself that
> nourishes, energizes, and fully develops your God-given gifts.
>
> —ARCHANGEL MICHAEL

Allow these words to wash over you. Rest with them for a few minutes and feel your whole being come into alignment with their truth. Do this for a few minutes. You have now opened a conduit to the wisdom radiating from the author of tonight's contemplation—Archangel Michael. Open your eyes and continue tonight's session by performing the following dream exercise.

Tonight's Exercise: Dreaming for Others

Dreaming for others and interpreting your dream for its hidden message is a unique way to get answers from the invisible realms about another's concerns and situations. You could do this for a friend or just an interested person you know. Often the other person is too close to a situation to interpret the clues from the dream worlds. As a result their dream messages go unrecognized. You can have a dream for another tonight by using the following technique.

1. Upon retiring for the evening, relax. Close your eyes and use your imagination to visualize the person you wish to dream for.

2. With your attention on that person's form, say the following affirmation:

   I ask all aspects of my being, including my soul self, the angels, and archangels to send me a dream message to help _____ (state the person's name). I will remember and understand the hidden messages of my dreams.

Repeat this affirmation several times. With each repetition feel Archangel Michael's presence grow stronger and closer. As you drift off to sleep, rest easy knowing that Michael will lead you in your dream world journey tonight.

Upon awakening in the morning, remember to lie still and keep your eyes closed. Focus your attention on accessing your dream memories. Take some time to allow your dream memories to impress themselves upon your waking mind. After a few minutes, record your dreams in your journal.

When you have finished, begin to unseal the messages hidden within your dreams. Call upon Archangel Michael to bring you insight as you interpret your dreams by saying the following prayer of invocation.

Dear Archangel Michael,
   Please shine your light of truth upon my dream messages.
Help me to unseal their wisdom from a position of clarity,
understanding, and compassion. Amen.

Next, perform all seven steps of the interpretation process. The seven steps (from chapter 3) are repeated for you below:

1. Make an inventory or list of each of the characters that appear in your dream, both human and nonhuman.

2. Examine both your feelings and the feelings of the dream client toward the dream characters.

3. Examine the dream client's role in the dream and his or her relationships to the dream characters.

4. Review the actions taking place in the dream.

5. Find out what aspect of the dream client the dream characters represent by having the dream client engage them in imaginary conversation.

6. Analyze the dream setting (location/time of day/environment).

7. Consider the current life situation of the dream client.

Be sure to include the dream client's input as you formulate the dream message. You will know that you have arrived at the correct dream interpretation when you feel something "click" within you. Don't be discouraged if this doesn't happen right away. The message of your dream may become unsealed over the course of the day or it may take even more time to emerge.

Visiting Heaven

Over the past twenty-nine days you have learned much about yourself. You've learned about the segments of the self that compose your inner being; the importance of discovering and accomplishing your life's mission; and how to use your dream worlds to increase your awareness of your soul's purpose and pattern for this lifetime on earth. Your newly gained knowledge will help you to fulfill your special piece in the puzzle of life.

Tonight you will have the opportunity to visit the realms of the angels, perhaps even to see where you will live and have your being in the afterlife. During your visit to heaven, you may encounter loved ones who have passed on. You may also be shown a vision of how your life can reflect the peace and love that is present at all times in the heavenly worlds.

Humans have long sought the elusive state of peace and tranquility. Wars have been fought and many have suffered through humanity's ignorance of the spiritual reality of life. If we really knew that beyond this mortal world lay another world—a much finer world where there is only light and love—we would put aside our differences and work to spread the unity of heaven to all who live upon the earth.

We are all connected, one to the other, in God's love and in His design. Like pieces of a puzzle fit together to form a bigger picture, our lives fit together with all others to form the picture of God's creation. Just as a puzzle's pieces cannot be forced together, we cannot force our life to fit where it is not designed to fit.

In the heavenly worlds all the separate pieces of God's creation fit together perfectly and without effort. There is no hunger, no want, no war. In heaven there are no words of harm spoken nor hurt felt. All of the virtues exemplified by the four archangels, especially truth, wholeness, strength, and love, are magnified and found in the souls that reside there. In heaven we find only beauty.

In the heavenly worlds one can always hear the gentle sound of God's music moving through the air, softly flowing like a meandering forest stream.

Love flows there, as abundant and free as the air here on earth. It is all around. The light of God surrounds and infuses each heavenly being in a glorious halo. Consider the following description from the book of Revelation.

> And the twelve gates were twelve pearls; every several gate was of one pearl: and the street of the city was pure gold, as it were transparent glass. I did not see a temple in the city, because its temple is the Lord God Almighty and the Lamb. And the city has no need of sun or moon to light it, for the glory of God and of the Lamb illuminate it.
>
> —REV. 21:21–23

In heaven we will have the opportunity to continue our advancement in areas that interest us, whether in creative arts, such as music, writing, or painting, or scientific pursuit, such as experimenting with the elements that God has used to manifest creation. All actions, whether individual or group, work together in union to serve the Creator and all creation.

Heaven is not just a place, it is a state of consciousness. As a state of consciousness, heaven can be experienced by each of us—here and now. If you have ever wondered what heaven is like, you can find out in your dreams worlds tonight. Tonight's exercise is designed to stimulate a dream of heaven. Your dream experience may include a meeting with a loved one, a holy encounter with a saint, or even an audience with God Himself!

Attuning Your Consciousness to the Guiding Angel

Uriel, archangel of love, beauty, and awareness, will be your guide tonight during your journey into the dream worlds. Before performing tonight's dream exercise, use the following invocation and contemplation to attune yourself to his holy presence.

Invocation to Archangel Uriel

> *Uriel, holy angel of God,*
>   *Come to me tonight. May your peaceful presence lead me to a deeper appreciation of my dream worlds. Help me to understand and integrate all parts of myself so that I may live a life rooted in love and joy once again. Let my decisions be based on love, not fear; and let my every action contribute to the never-ending demonstration of the Creator's love for all life. Amen.*

Allow yourself to feel Uriel's presence enter your heart. Next, to further attune your consciousness to the guiding presence for tonight, read and contemplate the following words.

> Honor the truth of each perspective because it is verily one of the layers of truth. As we peel away the layers of truth, so shall we reveal God's ultimate truth.
>
> —Archangel Uriel

Allow these words to wash over you. Rest with them for a few minutes and feel your whole being come into alignment with their truth. Do this for a few minutes. You have now opened a conduit to the wisdom radiating from the author of tonight's contemplation—Archangel Uriel. Open your eyes and continue tonight's session by performing the following dream exercise.

Tonight's Exercise: Visiting Heaven

Can you remember a time when the beauty of God's creation filled you with awe? Perhaps you were watching a sunset on the beach or a sunrise in the mountains. As beautiful as those scenes may have been, they only reflect a small fraction of the beauty that awaits you in heaven. Contrary to popular belief, you don't need to wait until death to visit the heavenly realms. You can visit them tonight in your dreams. Upon retiring for sleep tonight try the following technique.

1. Take a few moments to visualize the most beautiful place you have ever visited. Imagine being there once again and allow yourself to re-experience it using as many senses as you can. Take your time and become fully present within the scene. Appreciate deeply the beauty that you are now viewing.

2. Repeat the following affirmation as you drift off to sleep:

Archangel Uriel will show me the heavenly worlds tonight in my dreams.

As you repeat this affirmation, feel the presence of Archangel Uriel growing stronger and closer. Continue to repeat the affirmation and gently relax into a deep and restful sleep, knowing that soon you will be given a glimpse of the glorious heavenly realms of God.

Upon awakening in the morning, remember to lie still and keep your eyes closed. Focus your attention on accessing your dream memories. Take some time to allow your dream memories to impress themselves upon your waking mind. After a few minutes, record your dreams in your journal.

When you have finished, begin to unseal the messages hidden within your dreams. Call upon Archangel Uriel to bring you insight as you interpret your dreams by saying the following prayer of invocation.

> *Dear Archangel Uriel,*
>   *Be with me now as I uncover the hidden meaning of my dreams. I invoke your joyful and loving presence to help me see and appreciate all that I experience within the dream worlds, and all that I experience in my present life. Amen.*

Next, perform all seven steps of the interpretation process. The seven steps (from chapter 3) are repeated for you below:

1. Make an inventory or list of each of the characters that appear in your dream, both human and nonhuman.
2. Examine your feelings about the dream characters.
3. Examine your role in the dream and your relationships to the dream characters.
4. Review the actions taking place in the dream.
5. Find out what aspect of yourself the dream characters represent by engaging them in imaginary conversation.
6. Analyze the dream setting (location/time of day/environment).
7. Consider your current life situation.

You will know that you have arrived at the correct dream interpretation when you feel something "click" within you. Don't be discouraged if this doesn't happen right away. The message of your dream may become unsealed over the course of the day or it may take even more time to emerge as you work through your spiritual growth issues.

CHAPTER 5

Journey's End

We hope you have enjoyed exploring your dream worlds with the help of the archangels. Even though your journey has ended, you can continue to explore and chart your dream worlds if you so desire. Just make a new journal and re-dedicate yourself to the thirty-day process once again. You can run through a thirty-day dream cycle as often as you wish.

Remember that the archangels carry messages from God to you, and that your growth and expansion is very important to them. Archangel Michael can be with you in an instant. Call upon him to help you see the truth of who you are—the truth that is revealed to you nightly in your dreams. Call upon Raphael, archangel of healing, wholeness, and acceptance, and he will bring dreams of acceptance and integration into your life. Gabriel will remind you of your life purpose—your reason for being here now upon the earth plane. Call upon him and he will walk with you in your dreams, guiding you toward alignment with your soul and your mission for this lifetime. And don't forget to call upon Uriel, the archangel of love, beauty, and awareness. He will help you to appreciate, with a joyful spirit, the gift that each day's learning will bring to you as you explore and chart your dream worlds.

The Dream Journey Summary

There is one final step for you to complete that will assist you in assimilating the experiences and insights of the past thirty days. This step consists of reviewing and summarizing your dreams. Take some time to go over your dreams and then use your dream journal to record your answers to the questions below. Answer the questions as best you can. Studying your responses can help you to identify personal patterns that may be holding you in cycles of self-limitation. This new understanding will empower you to consciously choose a new belief system—one that will challenge you to incorporate beliefs that will help you live life to the fullest each day.

1. What common themes, symbols, and characters can you identify from your dreams over the past thirty days?

2. What did you learn about your personal patterns/emotional issues in the past thirty days?

3. Which of the angels/archangels/spirit guides appeared most often in your dream worlds? What do their unique qualities/virtues have to teach you about yourself?

4. What did you learn about your connection to the angelic realms in the past thirty days?

5. Based on your thirty-day dream journey, what qualities do you need to bring from within to help you accomplish your mission for this lifetime?

6. What steps are you now prepared to take toward accomplishing your life's mission?

Through your efforts to understand yourself and your life experiences, you will find your ability to correctly interpret your dreams increases dramatically. This will improve your self-confidence and bring balance into your outer life. The importance of this ability should not be underestimated. Dreams provide us with crucial information that we can use in our waking world to fulfill our purpose, expand our creativity, and keep our hearts open to the Holy Spirit.

A New Paradigm for the New Millennium

As humanity reaches into the new millennium we can each choose to begin a cycle of concentrated self-development and growth. Collectively this will result in a new paradigm—and the "new age" spoken of for so long will finally become a common reality. It will be a new age of honesty, truthful expression, and constructive accomplishment.

You are a unique and important part of God's creation. There is not another being anywhere who is exactly like you, nor will anyone's gifts manifest exactly as yours will here on the earth plane. No path or guru holds the complete key to the mystery of life or to the dream worlds. Why? Because the nature of life is to continuously expand and unfold in ever-changing patterns.

Each one of us plays a crucial role in the unfoldment of the universe. Like the individual threads of a tapestry, each of us is necessary for the design of life to be woven properly. Each one of us holds a piece of the overall puzzle of life, and the tapestry will only be as strong, beautiful, and true as the individual threads from which it is composed.

Throughout our lives we play a dual role: that of student and teacher. Our greatest learning usually occurs when we courageously assume the role of teacher. This applies to dream world learning as well, so please allow yourself to share with others the pearls of wisdom you are so carefully gathering on your life journey.

What is the ultimate purpose of our dream world exploration? We dream to promote healing and unity, which brings God's greatest gift—His love—into manifestation upon the earth. We each are co-workers with God. We share His mighty love force by integrating our self-segments, coming into alignment with our soul's purpose, and dedicating our lives to loving each other as honestly, as deeply, and as purely as we can.

Remember that the archangels can be with you even after your journey is complete—you have only to consciously invoke their presence. As messengers of God they care deeply about you and all of humanity. Their light and love is always available to you as you move forward in your life journey—charting and exploring the worlds of mind and spirit.

The Circle of Angelic Enlightenment

Only a few times during our life does a window of expanded consciousness open up to our awareness. It was at just such a time during September of 1994 when Linda and Peter first met. Events converged at the first WE (Walk-ins for Evolution) conference in St. Paul, Minnesota. A circle of light was formed as Linda and Peter joined together to fulfill their destiny in the service of the angels and the Creator.

Linda and Peter founded The Circle of Angelic Enlightenment to serve as a vehicle for the Archangels' Plan of Healing to reach the world. The Circle is dedicated to assisting individuals in their efforts to define and accomplish their life's mission. Through the inspiration and guidance of the angels and the archangels, Linda and Peter present the Archangels' Plan of Healing through books, tapes, Soul Name Songs™, angel study courses, and angel readings.

For more information on their services, the study/membership program, speaking engagements, or private sessions, you can reach Linda and Peter by e-mailing them at:

The Circle of Angelic Enlightenment
Email: info@angelic-circle.com
Web Site: www.angelic-circle.com